life
after
sexual abuse

life
after
sexual abuse

A Practical
Healing Toolkit
to Reconnect
Mind, Body & Soul

STACIE GLASS

tgh.

LONDON

Life After Sexual Abuse: A Practical Healing Toolkit to Reconnect Mind, Body & Soul

The information given in this book should not be treated as a substitute for professional medical advice. Always consult a medical practitioner.

Although the author and publisher have made every effort to ensure that the information in this book was correct at press time, the author and publisher do not assume and hereby disclaim any liability to any party for any loss, damage, or disruption caused by errors or omissions, whether such errors or omissions result from negligence, accident, or any other cause.

The book information is catalogued as follows;
Author Name(s): Stacie Glass
Title: Life After Sexual Abuse: A Practical Healing Toolkit to Reconnect Mind, Body & Soul

Description; First Edition
1st Edition, 2021

Book Design by Leah Kent

ISBN 978-1-914447-19-8 (paperback)
ISBN 978-1-914447-20-4 (ebook)

Published by That Guy's House
www.ThatGuysHouse.com

To my inner child – thank you for all you endured, your strength and resilience.

I am here because of you.

CONTENTS

Foreword

Experiencing sexual abuse, rape and childhood sexual abuse is life changing. Many survivors struggle to acknowledge what has happened to them and how to cope with the aftermath of abuse. There is not a path to follow that suits everyone, there is no prescription that can wipe away the memories. As a survivor of incest myself, I could not make sense of what had happened to me and why. Now as an adult of mature years I have learnt that my journey is unique and my search for healing is never complete, but it is my journey and I am content with that.

In this book, you have found a friend. Stacie shares with you her story and she takes you gently by the hand through where she has been and where you may be just starting. There is no path you cannot travel, as she explains ways for you to deal with the memories that hold you back.

Each chapter opens up to speak to you as you are now, but also as the person who experienced a terrible trauma. Stacie reaches out to you gently, describing ways that have helped her when she was over-whelmed. She connects with the 'inner child' who was not loved or cared for. Perhaps remembering the child you were is too difficult; in this book you will find a way to connect and to love that little person. You may wish to read this book and then to put it down to come back to sometime later. Stacie gives you permission to do this. In fact, the key to your healing is to recognise that you have the power and the right to make your own way through.

In my life as a survivor, a midwife and a psychother-apist, I have been privileged to walk with many sur-vivors on their path to healing. I have witnessed the desperate, raw emotions of someone standing strong in the memories of their past. This book will be an important resource for survivors and therapists. However, it is more than a toolkit for recovery. It is a book that is full of love and hope. It is a love letter to you for all that you lost and all that you were denied. Stacie has been on her own journey of heal-ing, and she is holding out her arms for you now to follow your own path to healing.

Dr Kathryn Gutteridge

Introduction

What does life after sexual abuse mean to you? What would it look like?

What does healing feel like and how will you know you are healing?

When I started my healing journey a decade ago, there weren't any books that described life after sexual abuse and what could help in the mammoth task to feel 'normal' again. I have come to realise that these past 10 years have been the start of the journey to call back the pieces of myself; I am not broken and I am worthy of a wholesome and fulfilling life.

I am enough exactly as I am, and so are you.

What does 'healing' mean? We will explore this throughout this book with ways you can begin healing or take you further on your path. This book is intended to support and encourage you to learn what feels right for you. I encourage self-inquiry to find out what 'healing' means to you. The general meaning of the word is 'the process of becoming well again'. My interpretation of the word is bringing balance to mind, body and soul, and to know and understand ourselves with acceptance, forgiveness and compassion.

You are not what happened to you.

You are so much more and you deserve so much more.

It takes a lot of courage and sometimes several attempts to begin the healing journey. I know from my personal experience that avoiding the shadow and pain of our trauma only enables it to keep showing up, getting louder and louder until we listen to what it wants us to hear, see and feel. If we don't listen, it shows up repeatedly, ever more present in ways that cannot be ignored.

Healing happens when we face the shadow and triggers of the trauma, moving through the pain, the pattern and the story, and choosing a new direction. Healing is a process, one we can't predict nor control but is one that is unique to us and our individual needs. Healing happens when we choose to want more, choosing ourselves.

A Letter to You

Dear reader,

I see you. Thank you for choosing to read this labour of love and healing.

It is my hope that you find something within these pages to help you on your journey.

These pages begin by describing my journey from feeling lost, numb, broken, shameful and guilty because I was sexually abused and raped aged 11-13. At aged 26, I began my healing journey to break down those burdens I carried, to set myself free and to come home to myself. I didn't realise then that I was on a self-discovery expedition but that led me to these pages now; with a passion to speak up loudly and clearly for others who don't feel yet able to speak their truth. If you are reading this, you too may be on this tumultuous path or maybe you are supporting someone who has been sexually abused. It isn't easy, so my advice is that you take this book at your own pace. One thing I learned early on in my therapy was that I didn't hold myself with care or love, and the past 10 years have been about learning how to do that. And so, my wish for you is that if this sounds familiar, this is permission to hold yourself with care and love – because you so deserve it.

You are more courageous than you know.

Pause when you need to.

Stop when you need to.

Come along with me and I will help you feel hopeful and inspired to heal for you – you are worthy and you deserve the life you dream of. Healing after any trauma can feel like standing at the bottom of a mountain, staring up, unable to see the summit and feeling like getting there is impossible. I'm here to tell you that taking that first step up the mountain is what healing is. Wanting more for yourself is healing. We each have our own mountain and the landscape will be different for each of us. How one person takes the journey is unique in every sense because how they got to the bottom of the mountain was unique to them.

Is healing after sexual abuse hard? Yes.

Is it worth it? YES.

If 10 years ago I knew what I now know, I would have started this process sooner, but I believe we are where we are meant to be and we start when we feel ready. It's okay if you don't yet feel ready.

I want to be clear from the outset that this is my personal journey and it is not my intention to preach to anyone – only you know what is best for you individually, but it is my intention to offer hope that life after sexual abuse does exist and that the practical healing toolkit I outline in this book opens up doorways and avenues for your own healing, exploring what that looks and feels like for you. Be curious and give yourself permission to try different things. And give yourself permission to rest when you need to.

Thank you for picking this book up; the fact you have shows that you are ready to explore your healing and to put yourself first – for you.

I appreciate you.

With love,

Stacie

Recent worldwide statistics from The World Health Organisation (WHO, 2021) showed that one in three women have experienced physical and/or sexual violence by a partner or sexual violence by a non-partner. The majority of these was abuse from an intimate partner, and therefore the perpetrators were not strangers. Internationally, about 20% of women report being victims of sexual violence as children. This figure is predicted to be much higher, considering that many survivors do not go on to disclose their trauma to anyone. This is especially true for male survivors. Shame and guilt keep people trapped into secrecy and is one reason for my drive to write openly about it, for those who are suffering in silence.

You are not alone and you deserve to be free from the pain.

I want to give a special mention here to all survivors; men, women, transgender, non-binary and hetero/homosexual people … we are all humans, regardless of gender, race, culture, and sexual orientation. If you have experienced sexual trauma or support a survivor, you are welcome here. Sexual abuse affects anyone and everyone; our experiences (and the challenges of these) will be unique, as we all are as humans, but I want this to be a safe space for all survivors to feel seen, heard, and held in unity. I can only talk about my own sexual abuse experience as a white, British heterosexual, cisgendered female and will only ever be an expert in my personal experience.

However, one thing we all share is the sheer strength, bravery, and resilience to survive sexual trauma. You have survived something so unspeakable and painful.

I honour each and every one of you.

How to Read This Book

I recommend that you buy yourself a beautiful notebook and pen to dedicate to your healing journey. Writing is such a therapeutic process – there are no rules for how you do this. A cornerstone of this book is the writing practice of journaling.

I offer some journal prompts that are a guide for self-inquiry. These are meant to be supportive so take what resonates and leave what doesn't. Anything I suggest in this book is exactly that – suggestions. I hope there is something helpful for you within these pages, even if it is the curiosity to explore other things that go on to help you heal.

This is your journey and there isn't a grand finale where you get 'I am healed' status. So, make the process, your process, sacred.

The word 'sacred' means 'regarded with great respect and reverence', and in the words of a favourite author and meditation teacher Sarah Blondin – 'To make your life sacred means to hold your life as an exquisite masterpiece.'

Life's trials and tribulations are all sacred because our journey is unique.

Nothing is for certain but something has been given to us – life

So, what do you want to do with this gift of this precious life?

Can you hold yourself in the times of desolation as equally as in the times of joy?

Growth and transformation follow the darkest of days.

I suggest that you consider how you will know when you are healing – how will you feel different? Will you look different?

What is your intention for your healing journey?

One thing I encourage you to do is to make a commitment to yourself, for yourself.

There are two terms in this book that I use – 'survivor' and 'journey' that don't fully land with me, but they are the best terms I can find, so know that if any of the 'labels' I use throughout do not fit perfectly for you, replace them with ones that do. The reason why I use the term 'survivor' is because I know I have survived my worst days, and no matter what comes my way, I know I've survived something incredibly traumatic and despite that I'm here. So yes, I am a survivor. If you are reading this then you, too, are a survivor (or someone who supports a survivor) – maybe of past sexual abuse or maybe of another physical/psychological trauma.

The word 'journey' implies there is a final destination that we magically arrive at and miraculously, we are healed. This may very well happen – one thing I know from being on my own healing journey is that it has changed my outlook on life, opening up endless possibilities where before, there wasn't even a glimmer of hope. The healing journey takes you where you need to go and be; an inward quest to find peace and self. How long will it take? No one knows, but it takes as long as you need. Be curious as to where the path will take you, trust your intuition, lean into what feels nourishing and give yourself permission to release what no longer serves you. There is no grand finale to healing and that is because we are meant to evolve and flourish. But the question is, will you allow yourself to do so? Will you allow the healing to happen as it needs to, as opposed to how you think it 'should' be? I know this question well. For a long time, I was seeking ways to be 'fixed' and for it to all disappear and be 'done'. But now, I understand that healing happens whilst in the process, and each step adds up to progress. Honour the process and your progress.

This book does not mean that that I am healed and what worked for me will miraculously help you – only you can do that – but know, I am healing along-side you. I am healing every day. I will continue to navigate my emotions, my grief and trauma wounds that this experience brought me, but I took back my power when I chose myself. The ultimate destination is not 'I am healed', it is the ability to live a life full of possibilities without your past having power over you or holding you back. I know my trauma is part of my human fabric. It was once a painful wound, but after reclaiming my power and the pieces of myself, I now see it as 'Kintsugi' – the Japanese art of putting broken pottery pieces back together with gold. For this to happen, an inner shift needs to take place. There needs to be a want and a will to take steps in a direction where fear lies. Fear is the human protective mode which is needed for so many reasons but it also has the ability to overwhelm us and keep us small. Once we acknowledge and face the fear, it loses its power to hold us stuck where we are.

Each chapter begins with a letter to my inner child; my healing journey has enabled me to reconnect to her – my inner warrior that survived so much. It is something I suggest you try for yourself. It is a practice that facilitates greater compassion and understanding towards ourselves – this is such a necessary part of any healing process.

Chapter 1 is my journey of how I got here. I talk about my experience of sexual trauma – you will learn there that there wasn't a magic wand that I was fortunate to find. I had to look within to find my strength to dig deep and call upon the resilience I already had from getting through the trauma. Then, there is a 'Healing Diary' section which has entries from the diary I kept during my many days in talking therapy. I also outline how journaling is different and how you can approach this practice to gain insight into your inner world. Think of it as free therapy but also as a way to build a relationship with yourself.

Chapters 2, 3, and 4 are the heart of this book: how healing mind, body and soul are integral to reconnecting to self after trauma and is the foundation for healing. In each chapter, I start with a vulnerable letter to my inner child, a practice that in itself can be deeply healing, as we reconnect to that part of ourselves that we unconsciously disconnect from in order to survive. This book is a combination of my story, my experience, but also theory and professional understanding of the mind-body connection.

Most of all, I wanted to write a book that is practical in the field of healing after sexual trauma from the perspective of someone that has walked the path, and so in each chapter, there are 'Healing Toolkit' suggestions that have helped me. There isn't a manual that can outline 'do this and you will be healed', and this is because we are all unique and have unique needs. So, although this is to give an insight for what may help, my main intention is to encourage self-inquiry and seek out what will help you, because only you know that.

Chapter 5 is the golden thread throughout and such a pivotal part of healing after sexual trauma: self-love and compassion. In this chapter, most importantly I invite you to explore what self-love means to you and why this is so key to your journey home to yourself. Chapter 6 is about support, specifically for those who support survivors during the healing journey – this is to recognise how the effects of sexual trauma are far-reaching and the significance of supporting the survivor in the most helpful way for them. Supporters need support too and that is honoured in that chapter. Each chapter is finished with what I hope to be helpful self-inquiry journal prompts. These are questions that have either helped me throughout my journey so far or ones that I feel would have been insightful if I had explored this writing practice 10 years ago.

Read this book in the way that feels right for you. It is divided into chapters so it can be read in sections or it can be read from start to finish, but what is important to me, is that you read it in the most helpful way for you. Your power and control were taken from you before, and my wish is that this book is a permission slip to take back your power and heal your way. I have also curated a list of 'things I wish I knew' for you to refer to when you need some gentle, loving reminders that can be used as affirmations or love notes to leave around your home. There will be days when it all feels too much – they are part of the process, so know that those are also steps forward, even though they won't feel like it. For the dark cloud days, I have suggested a 'them days' section for you to fill in so that you or your supporters can refer to it, which may help get you through a little bit gentler. You can access PDF versions of these from my website: **www.stacie-glass.com/lifeaftersexualabuse.**

This book is written from my heart and I hope it meets you where you are and guides you to where you want to be. We can't change the past, however much we wish we could, but we can begin healing the imprints and scars that trauma leaves upon our mind, body, and soul. The important thing is that you know what healing means to you and take steps towards that goal – it isn't a destination, it's a sense of wellbeing and liberation. You are worthy. Yes, you.

You are not alone.

My vision for journeying with you goes beyond the pages of this book. This is your journey, so choose who you want to take along with you.

There are ways you can bring me along if you choose...

Website

Visit my website to see everything in one place and connect with me personally if you feel called to: **www.Stacie-Glass.com**

....

In May 2017, I started a Facebook blog to share my journey in the hope of helping others who were feeling alone – I share candid videos about my experience.

Facebook

Life after sexual abuse
facebook.com/CSAblog/

Instagram

@_StacieGlass_
#lifeaftersexualabuse

Healing Diary

Diary Entries From My Time in Therapy

Here are diary entries that I wrote when I started therapy in 2011 that I have copied directly; this is a realistic insight into how I was feeling at the time. I have included these so that you may see something similar to how you feel or what you are experiencing, to know you are not alone. Although we each have unique experiences of sexual trauma, one thing I've noticed from talking to other survivors is that how it makes us feel is similar – the isolation, depression, guilt, and shame, which are just a few of the overwhelming things we can feel. I don't claim that healing is easy – it is messy and it is painful but what I hope is that you see that it is worth it. As you read this section, be gentle with yourself if it is bringing up difficult emotions for you – come back to it or skip until the 'Healing Toolkit' part. This section is intended to be helpful for you to recognise that you are not alone.

Whilst reading this section, notice what comes up for you and what the similarities and differences are to your own experience – write it all down. This is not to make a direct comparison; but as a way to start to notice and acknowledge your experience. It is through acknowledging and honouring our experience exactly as it is that healing can occur. All of our experiences are valid. One of the main healing tools I highlight throughout this book is that of writing therapy – journaling to get a deeper insight into your inner world to process and release to facilitate healing.

At the end of this section, I describe what journaling is (and isn't) and the benefit of this practice during the healing process.

....

Wednesday 3rd August 2011

I have had a few more therapy sessions – they have been quite upsetting but I know they part of a necessary process I need to go through. I have begun to explore uncomfortable feelings about the past and the therapist is helping me to make sense of how the past is affecting me now. I never imagined things would get to this from suppressing my thoughts and emotions, however, I now realise it is a necessary process to regain control of my life and to move forward. I feel better in myself now but I don't think that the tablets are helping to level my mood. I am going back to Dr C tomorrow to talk about the tablets. It's my 26th birthday in 3 days ... my aim is by my 27th birthday to feel I can accept my past and to feel stronger for dealing with this now so it doesn't continue to affect my life.

Friday 26th August 2011

I enjoyed my birthday despite how I'm feeling internally. It's like I have so much darkness inside. I know this darkness is not mine to carry and it is time to release it. I'm now on my 3rd type of anti-depressant after the others not suiting me. My sleep continues to be disturbed – I am having unusual and scary dreams – it's as if my subconscious is trying to tell my conscious mind something...

I had another therapy session Wednesday after having a break last week. Prior to the session, I was debating whether the therapy is even helping; however, during the session I realised what has improved – I am now able to talk about what happened more easily and without trying to suppress it. It frustrates me that I can't remember everything ... I understand this is a protective mechanism of my brain, but I feel there are pieces of a puzzle missing. Up until now, I've been ignoring the pieces, but now I want to complete the puzzle so that I can put it into a box, close the lid and store the box – contain it until when/if I want to access it again. Once it is in the box and contained, then it can't unexpectedly jump out at me – I can choose to be in control.

Tuesday 30th August 2011

I'm losing track of my days – I keep getting confused. Time is passing by so quickly and I can't believe I've now been off work for 11 weeks, it feels more like 11 days. Even after this time I still can't imagine going back to work and living 'normally'. I don't think I recognised until recently that I am unwell. I recognised I felt deeply sad but the array of emotions I'm feeling can't express the darkness I feel inside. I am mentally and emotionally unwell and I need really recognise and honour where I am at. Wishing I was further forward is not going to get me there. Although I'm feeling more positive than I have been, I feel incredibly irritable and I just want to be alone. I can't remember the last time I last slept undisturbed. Maybe I never will sleep well again now the emotional lid is off.

Wednesday 31st August 2011

Another therapy session today. This past week has been best and the worst – positive because I have realised a lot in this time and seeing progress with my sessions – negative because I have been ultra-irritable and getting angry very easily. I think the anger is coming from the suppressed emotions I have about what happened to me – it's been suppressed for so long and now it's getting a chance to make itself heard. I know this sense of depression is causing me to be selfish but I know that this time is for me – it is OK for me to be angry, upset, sad, irritated, frustrated, and grieved and anything in between. No one can tell me how to feel or tell me to cheer up/get on with life because it happened to ME. I need empathy and space to do what I need to do to feel myself again and maybe become a totally different version of myself. What I do know is that I need to focus on making myself better because I only have this life now, and the first 25 years of my life certainly weren't the best. I have a chance to *make the next 25 years be of a life I deserve. No one can tell me how to feel or 'fix' this for me.*

'Even the darkest night will end
and the sun will rise again.'

~ Victor Hugo ~

Below is a letter that I wrote to one of my abuser's during a time that I was processing anger. Anger was an emotion I particularly struggled to process. It was trapped within my body but through writing I found an outlet:

....

A LETTER TO 'HIM'

I am angry because I said no – you took my choice away.

I am angry because I was a child and defenceless.

I am angry because I cannot change what happened to me.

I am angry because you made me feel ashamed and guilty – it wasn't my fault – it makes me angry you made me feel that it was.

It makes me angry that you fully intended and planned forcing it against my will.

It disgusts me that you could deny what you did – I can't ever forget.

I am angry that I can't change what you did.

I am angry that you cannot see the consequences of what you did to me.

I am angry that you took away my childhood.

I am angry at the effect your actions have had upon my life, but it ended for you the moment you left me that night.

I am angry because I felt so alone with a terrible secret.

I am angry because it is NOT okay – it's not okay that I should have to accept what you did.

....

Reflections Now

I tried to keep a regular journal, but I found it exhausting committing to a daily practice and at times it felt like a 'dear diary' thing, so I didn't write as often as I wanted to. There is a big difference between keeping a diary and a journal. A diary describes daily details such as what you did that day, whilst keeping a journal goes deeper into your inner world, revealing insights and allowing space to process difficult emotions.

Looking back at my writing during my early therapy days, it was helpful to describe how I was feeling then, but I wish I knew more about journaling and how that could have complimented my talking therapy. I hadn't looked back upon this diary until I came to write this book (10 years later) – it has been so insightful and healing. Reading it was like being transported in time to the darkest of days. It took me right back to that time, but what was beautiful is how despite feeling emotional at times, I was able to hold my inner child and remind her that she is safe now. The worry about writing such a book is that it raises the question: Am I ready? Will it trigger me? The process of writing this book has showed me that this is a full circle moment; I am ready because I put the work in. It was pure grit and hard work, but it was so worth it. I feel I have called back those missing pieces of myself and now I look back with tenderness and pride. I am still 'healing in progress' and probably always will be – and that's okay. I am so grateful that I am where I am now, living a life that I deserve and knowing that the work I have put in has taken the power out of my traumatic experience and redirected to self-healing.

I explain that I had some resistance to writing a journal at the time of going through therapy and I remember it well, but my reflection now is that I wish I wrote more. Writing down your thoughts and feelings on paper makes them more tangible and it's a way of processing, moving out of the conscious mind and into the subconscious (see more about this in Chapter 2: Healing the Mind). I can see the process that I was going through and how insights were revealing themselves to me that probably wouldn't have the opportunity if I hadn't written them down. I encourage anyone at this phase of their healing to write as much as you can or draw/doodle – whatever you feel drawn to do. Let it all out. Your future self with be grateful you did.

The point of this process is to express yourself – exactly where you are, as you are. Abuse in itself suppresses and oppresses your natural self-expression and your rights as a human being. Do what you need to do – you might not yet know what that is, but writing down the question, 'What do I need right now?' and answering it without questioning and judgement is one way of unfiltering yourself and discovering what you most need to heal. That may change each day – give yourself permission to change your mind. Give yourself permission to pause, to rest, and maybe you just need to 'be' today.

HEALING TOOLKIT

Journaling

Journaling can be used as a self-directed writing therapy, a tool to share our inner world and story about the trauma we went through. It creates the space and opportunity to remove ourselves from identifying with the trauma, moving into awareness that it was an experience we went through, but it is not who we are.

Research has shown journaling to have many health benefits, improving both physical and mental wellbeing by reducing stress levels. It is believed that the act of writing accesses the left brain, which is analytical and rational. While the left brain is occupied by writing, the right brain is free to create, intuit and feel. Therefore, writing removes mental blocks and allows us to use all of our brainpower to better understand our inner world, others, and the world around us.

Journaling is ...

A tool for self-expression – self-directed writing therapy.
Individual to you.

A gateway for healing and transformation.

A way to evolve our self-awareness and to improve our relationships with ourselves.

A way to tell our story exactly as we experience it and an opportunity to create new ones.

A way to release ourselves of intense emotions and thoughts.

A tool to organise our thoughts, behaviour, and our lives in general.

A tool for your future self to reflect back on your journey – celebrate the journey.

A safe space to write exactly how you feel without judgement … keep that self-critic in check!

Journaling does not …

Replace the intentional action you have to take in your life to see changes, healing and growth.

It doesn't have to be boring and dull – make it what you want it to be and what works for you.

It doesn't have to be written words – it can be doodles, colours or drawings (even if you can't draw like an artist!)

It doesn't have to be shared or spoken out loud – unless you want it to be.

It's okay if journaling isn't for you – find other ways of self-expression such as singing or dancing.

If you are new to journaling, here are some ways to get started:

Buy a journal/notebook and pen that you love and create a safe space where you feel comfortable to release what you need to onto the pages. Create time each day/week or whatever feels right for you, but the main thing is the commitment and intention you bring to it.

What does your intention and commitment look like? What do you want to achieve from this practice? For example, self-expression, a space and place to be fully you.

Show up for yourself. Write this intention and commitment on the first page of your journal so that you can keep coming back to the reminder when you need it.

Release any expectations of what it 'should' be or that you have to write perfectly. It is meant to be raw, unfiltered honest self-expression – give yourself permission to forget about spelling and grammar, and write freely.

Where do you begin? Wherever you want to – there aren't any rules, only the ones you want to make, but allow yourself to change your mind.

Write the date at the beginning of each session – your future self will be grateful for this when you can't remember specifics. So, grab your favourite drink and dive in ...

Suggested questions to try:

- What do I want out of this practice?
- I believe journaling will help me...
- Am I willing to commit time and energy to getting the most out of this practice?
- Am I willing to be gentle with myself when telling my story and writing out my inner world?
- Am I willing to look within, even when it's uncomfortable?
- Today, I feel...
- I give myself permission to...
- I always...
- I never...
- Today, I most need to know...

If what comes up for you is too painful to face alone, I encourage you to talk to someone that you trust – a loved one or a therapist. You do not have to do this alone. You are not alone.

Through writing, you may just discover that your journal is an all-accepting, non-judgmental friend that you have long needed.

....

COURAGE

It is courageous to be where you are now

It is courageous to honour your past self
for getting you here

It is courageous to carry on each day

It is courageous to stay in bed today

It is courageous to sit with how you feel now

It is courageous to be willing to let go of the patterns
that you thought were keeping you safe

It is courageous to step away to look after yourself
when the feeling is too overwhelming

It is courageous to want more for your life

It is courageous to take it slow and even
pause when you need to

It is courageous to admit you don't
know what comes next.
No one does.

It is courageous to ask for help

It is courageous to want more for your future self

It is courageous to take baby steps forward

It is courageous to stay where you are for a while

You are courageous exactly as you are

I'm Not Broken

Hello dear one,

I am here with you now.

The 'journey' for me to realise that I had left you behind and to come back for you has been slow – I am here now and I am sorry. I am sorry I left you, I am sorry for what you went through. I am sorry you didn't get the love and support you deserved. I am sorry for the shame and guilt that was not yours to carry. I am sorry for your pain and sorrow. I want to honour the desolation, sorrow, shame, guilt and loneliness because they are valid – everything you felt was valid.

I want you to know that you are now safe and you are loved – you have always been loved. I know you didn't feel it then and I know it has taken me a long time to come back for you; I am here now. I am here to bring you along to reconnect us to wholeness; to tell you that you are not broken, we were never broken. To tell you that it was not your fault. I hear your fear to acknowledge and accept that it happened but my darling, this is the first step in the process, and fear tries to protect us but we have to face it. I am here to tell you we face the fear.

I first became aware of you, my inner child, when started talking therapy. It didn't happen immediately because I wasn't ready. You see, the beginning of therapy was brutal; it felt like the outer world was at battle with our inner world. I started therapy at the end of 2011 and I had no idea what to expect. It seems like such a blur now, but what I do remember are the tears. I cried each week for 6 months. I used to get frustrated that I cried so much, I couldn't understand why I just cried and had little words. Now, I know it was you telling me how it felt and that I had fully acknowledged and accepted what they did to us.

For so many years, I was successful at suppressing the memories because it just felt too raw and dark to let them fall out into my thoughts and consciousness. I now know it was a coping mechanism, but I also know in the long-term that it wasn't helpful for us to continue that way of living. That was holding us in fear, preventing us from healing and letting go of the shackles.

So, the river of tears was the start of when I realised I had left you behind and that to be able to move forward, I needed to go backwards in time to find you, to bring you along with me. At the time, I didn't understand what was happening because I was 'in' the process and that process involved going to the depths of the darkness we experienced and felt. They were the 6 months of tears where we retraced the past to enable us to feel what we felt. To no longer suppress but to give ourselves permission to feel in safety.

Initially, we needed a lot of encouragement and guidance from therapy; it created the safe space to allow us to let it all out. There was so much to release and it felt like a hurricane at sea. Crashing, falling, bruising, and ferocious but ultimately, it was powerful. We had to go through the storm to feel the power of the healing waters.

Healing is not a linear process; it was certainly an upward struggle in the beginning but now we ride the ebbs and flows. Now, I commit to continuation of this healing journey together. Please forgive me for taking so long to come back to you. I appreciate what you did for us and for that I am grateful and proud beyond words.

....

This chapter is the context for why I am writing a book about life after sexual abuse. As a survivor reading this chapter, be extra gentle with yourself – you might even want to skip past this one for now and come back to it when you feel you have the emotional capacity to read my story. My experience happened during childhood – my intention is to share my experience, in my own words and unfiltered. It isn't to hurt or upset anyone by telling my story; however, it is part of the healing process to be able to say exactly what happened to me and how it affected my life. I have the right to tell my story as I experienced it; there are of course, always more than one side of a story. This is mine. This is not a fictional story; this is my experience of sexual abuse and trauma.

Many survivors of sexual trauma never disclose what happened to them because of the fear of upsetting people they know. I understand this and there's no judgement if this is right for you. I feel strongly that we should be able to speak out about what happened, exactly as it happened without a filter because it happened to us.

For this chapter, I am putting others' feelings aside so that I may have my space to say what I needed to say for so long but was silenced.

I was silenced by the people who abused my human rights. I will not be silenced by anyone, anymore. We all deserve the right to speak up when what happened to us was so deeply wrong. When it is the right time.

I realise how hugely sensitive this topic is; I feel so passionate about getting more voices out there in society talking about something that generally is not talked about because it is 'too uncomfortable'. I agree and understand how difficult it is to even consider the prospect of a loved one having experienced sexual abuse, but it is even harder to be the person who has experienced it directly to go through what they did and then speak up about it. I have thought a lot about why it is difficult for society to talk about sex and sexual abuse and although I do recognise the complexities of talking about these 'taboo' topics, I cannot be complicit with or endorse keeping sexual abuse taboo because this only perpetuates it further. It is time society stands up for survivors. Abuse happens whether we talk about it or not and therefore, not talking about it continues to rob survivors of their right to live again, free of shame and guilt.

For many years, I remained silent about what happened to me and actually thought I would forever keep it a secret, and that was because I felt so ashamed and guilty that I 'allowed' it to happen. One thing that I find interesting talking to others that are at the beginning of their healing journey is that they often say, 'But I'm not brave enough.' I can relate to this because I was once a scared young woman, feeling unable to speak the words out loud with the fear of what might happen if I did, which prevented me from doing so. Yet, I am here now writing these words, hoping it may spark hope in others so that one day they may feel able to speak their truth, when it is right for them. What I do now know, is it takes time to feel ready and it's okay to not be ready yet. If this is you, be kind to yourself for not being ready yet, but know that you have it within you to be ready. Healing is possible; you are in control of your own healing.

So, how did I get here? My healing journey to date has spanned a decade and still counting. Healing isn't linear – it's more of a roller coaster or a squiggly line in all directions on a piece of paper. It will look different for each of us because we are unique – our experience was unique (to say the least) and how we heal will be unique. Something I have come to learn and accept is that I won't wake up one day and be 'healed'. The abuse I experienced will live with me in this lifetime but I no longer give it the power to control me or my life. I am able to look back and feel so much pride and reverence for my younger self. I am grateful for her strength and tenacity to survive and get me to this point. If you're at the beginning of your healing journey reading this, ask yourself what does healing look and feel like to you? How will you know when you've got there?

Early Years

My memory of my childhood is very patchy – trauma affects the brain and the memory (more on this in the next chapter). Whenever I've been asked about what my happiest childhood memories are, I struggle to answer. My childhood is not unique, and I recognise many children grow up in worse conditions. What I want to highlight here from the outset is that sexual abuse does not discriminate – it happens to those of all races, religions, cultures, ages and social circumstances.

I grew up living on council housing estates in Birmingham (UK) and we moved frequently so I don't think of any home as my family home. We didn't have much money, but we were never without food, clothes or a comfortable home. My parents separated before I was born, and I had an on/off relationship with my dad during my early years. I chose to break contact with him many years ago. I have two younger half siblings (my mother's children), with 6/8 years between us, so I didn't feel a close sibling relationship growing up. I have a half-sister that is my father's other daughter who I saw a lot of when we were younger; however, when her mum and our dad got divorced (she was 11 and I was 16), we lost contact and sadly, it was during this time she experienced her own sexual trauma.

Around the age of 11-13, I was sexually assaulted by my mother's then partner (M) and raped by his son (S); neither knew of the other's abuse. The sexual assault happened several times over a period of time whilst the rape was a one-off event. For many years I didn't recognise or accept what had happened to me. I suppressed the memories for a long time until I began remembering snippets as my understanding of what constitutes sexual assault and rape developed; I knew I needed to face what it all meant. I now understand that 'S' had been grooming me for several months – he was over the age of 16 and so was a few years older than me. He convinced me we were in a 'special' relationship. One night, he came around whilst I was babysitting my siblings who were in bed, and he raped me. I tried to fight him off unsuccessfully. His friend, who had driven him to the house, sat outside waiting, until he finished and they drove off; I didn't see him again after this. I internalised the belief that it was my fault because I didn't stop it from happening. I knew it was wrong but I took the blame inwards and blamed myself.

The inappropriate touching by 'M' occurred many times over a period of time. He was an alcoholic and would come home drunk and ask for cuddles on the sofa which actually meant his hands would touch my breasts. I was not developed in the breast area, which actually caused me much shame and a lack of confidence, so the fact he would do this only compounded my lack of self-esteem. I don't know where my mother was when this would happen, but she was not there and didn't know what was happening. I would usually try to make excuses or pretend to be asleep but, as any victim of abuse will know, these things don't perturb determined abusers.

I did attempt to tell both my parents, on separate occasions, within a year of the abuse happening, however, I wasn't taken seriously or believed. Sadly, this is quite common when abuse occurs within families. This meant that I had to continue to live with this man after disclosing what he had done to me until eventually, a few years later, my mother and 'M' broke up. The lack of belief from my parents has taken many years of emotional processing through therapy due to the grief of not being listened to and not having my best interests put first. What this has taught me is that parenting is not an automatic entitlement for being a biological parent; it is the love through action and effort that makes a person a parent.

I disclosed what happened to a few close friends during my teenage years but I wasn't yet ready to admit and acknowledge the full scale of what I had experienced. My inner child was so scared and so decided it was best to keep it a secret because I was 'bad' for letting it happen to me. As I was secondary school aged when the abuse happened, I remember going through school like a robot – physically there but not mentally or emotionally. My emotions seemed to be permanently switched off; I felt numb. I told my school best friend in a letter – no idea what I said but I didn't entertain any further discussion after the letter and that was the case with the few people I told throughout my early twenties. Maybe that was a sign of my inner child wanting to let it out, but the fear held me back from getting support and what would come next after admitting to myself that it happened to me.

On reflection now, I understand I was in 'protection mode', meaning I suppressed the memories, and I certainly didn't feel able to explore how the trauma had affected me. It was like a black box that I was actively trying to keep the lid firmly on, of the grief, shame, guilt and all the other complex emotions that come with trauma. They were bubbling up and trying to escape and with the passage of time, it was getting harder and harder to keep the lid on it all. I remember lots of periods throughout my teenage and young adult years feeling despair and depression but not understanding why. This was when my self-loathing and hatred was at its peak.

In 2007, my last year of university of my undergraduate degree, my best friend was writing her dissertation on the child birthing experiences of women who had experienced sexual abuse. I look back now and know this was a sign from the universe that this was something I needed and could get support for. So, I built the courage up to tell my best friend in a letter, explaining what had happened to me. I was more open to the conversation which started the dialogue about the potential for exploring the effects and maybe, there was an alternative to feeling the daily despair and depression.

I decided to reach out to my general practitioner (GP) doctor because I didn't know who else to ask for help but unfortunately, the disclosure made him freeze, unable to say much but sent me off with a hand-written phone number without an explanation; I didn't use the number. I was still unable to accept I had been raped and needed someone to validate my experience and guide me to support. This did not validate my experience and so I didn't call the phone number and tried to carry on with my life as I was before. I went through periods of depression on/off and didn't understand why – I felt trapped in my own mind and felt lonely in the secret and shame I was harbouring.

It took another 4 years until I was able to fully face what I kept inside for so long, believing it was my fault and not accepting the gravity of what had happened to me. In 2011, l had a better experience with a different GP who listened and validated my experience; he was also honest that he wasn't sure what support he could provide but was willing to learn and listen.

~ The response you receive
when disclosing abuse is critical to what
you do or do not do next. ~

I took several months off work, I started anti-depressants and I experienced sleep deprivation and mood
swings. I write about this within the diary entries in
the 'Healing Diary' section and within a few chapters, a window into how I was truly feeling at that
time. One thing I can say is that your memory does
fade of the hard times during healing. Now I look
back on these times with pride for my younger self
and her ability to be resilient and have the grit to
persevere.

Feel it even when it hurts ... every moment you're
sobbing or screaming, you're doing the work. Every
moment you're feeling, you're healing.

The only way out is through it.

It was when my sister gave me the number to Rape &
Sexual Violence Project (RSVP) West Midlands that
I felt ready to reach out and get the support I had
needed for so long. RSVP is a specialist charity that
provides compassionate support to sexual abuse sur-

vivors; calling them was one of my best life decisions so far. One thing I've learned is that you can't have any expectations for what your healing will look like or how long it will take. I remember feeling impatient that I wasn't 'fixed' yet ... 10 years later and now I know I was never broken, I just needed to call back the pieces of myself that were wrongly taken. That's where the premise for this book came from – learning that after any trauma, we can reconnect mind, body, and spirit and by doing so, we release the tight grip that the trauma has upon us.

I went to talking therapy over 6 years, every week for periods of 6 months. I am forever grateful to RSVP and their compassion and belief in me. I am particularly grateful to my therapist, Natalie, who nurtured me through it all: the pain, the tears, the moments of pride, and coming to the end of that chapter of my life. She inspired me to want more for my life and challenged me when I was accepting less than I deserved. She inspired me to get to this point in my own healing that I feel able to hold space for others through their vulnerability to be where they want to be.

The biggest thing I learnt from that process was that I didn't know what self-love and self-care were, and it gifted me understanding of how to start cultivating them – because I deserved them. Exploring self-love/self-care led me to finding several 'tools' to help me find and embrace my inner child, ultimately piecing the parts back together to feel my whole self. Healing isn't linear – it is like anything that we find challenging: high highs and deep lows. There are times we need to push ourselves forward to step out of our comfort zone and then are times we need to pause, rest and comfort ourselves. Facing the fear isn't easy – in fact, it is hard work – but I can attest to how worthwhile it is. The best decision I made was choosing me, choosing my peace, but ultimately wanting more for my life because … it wasn't my fault.

~ We can't change the past or the event but we can change how we feel about it and take back control of our lives. ~

Going to Court

I never thought I would ever tell a single person, never mind go to the police; so, the fact that I did still makes me think, 'Wow, anything really is possible' I hadn't ever considered it possible because it was historical abuse, but I gained the courage when my younger sister (who lived with her mum) told me in

2011 that she was sexually groomed by someone trusted in her extended family between the ages of 11-16 and had reported it to the police. This was before the time I had fully accepted and fully disclosed what happened to me so, as you can imagine, I was shocked and so sad that we both went through such trauma but were unable to support one another. She inspired me with her bravery to do such a hugely courageous thing, which made me question my long-held belief that I couldn't face my own inner wounds. Anyone who has ever been sexually abused will know the comfort that comes from talking to someone who similarly knows the pain of such a trauma. In an ideal world, sexual abuse would not exist, but in reality, in a world where it does, it helps to have support from both those who can directly relate from experience and also those who haven't had personal experience, but want to fiercely love and support us anyway.

The other motivating factor for me reporting what happened to me to the police was that I found out that 'S' had children. I knew that if I wanted to prevent anyone else from suffering the same trauma from him, I had to report it officially. I didn't want him to be a risk to his children or anyone else for that matter. I can't change what happened to me, but I didn't want anyone else to become his next victim.

The year 2015 had been a defining year in my life to date and it happened to be the year I turned 30. In that year when I went to court, one of my dear relatives died. I was studying full-time for a Master's degree and I was in an unhappy relationship; however, despite all that, throughout that year, I showed up for myself every week by going to my therapy sessions.

Going to court was terrifying but I channelled my inner child strength that got me through the process and we fought for justice. Historical abuse cases are notoriously difficult to achieve successful prosecution. My memory is a blur about the court experience and again I suspect that is because my mind was in protection mode, but what I do remember is how I felt, and that was terrified yet determined. It was my opportunity to say publicly what had happened and to let him know that it wasn't okay.

He was found guilty for sexual assault but the jury was unable to reach a unanimous 'guilty' for the rape charge. Following the verdict, I grieved for several weeks; I went through another layer of healing. It was like not being believed all over again. However, after allowing myself to feel, I recognised how far I had come to get to that point of standing up in a criminal court. I am deeply proud of myself for having the courage to stand up for my inner child; I healed so much from the process. I'm not an advocate for reporting to the police but I'm not against it either – I am an advocate for doing what you feel you need to do to heal. It isn't an easy process and you might not get the verdict you want from it, but if you have a strong sense for justice then it is worth considering.

Diary Entry: Saturday 13th June 2015

I haven't picked up this journal since I last wrote in it – it is now 2015 and a lot has changed. In April 2014, I reported to the police what happened to me – in August this year I will be going to court to face him just a few days after my 30th birthday. I am currently studying for a full time Master's degree and last month my beautiful aunty died. Her funeral is next week – I miss her so much. I have nearly completed another set of 24 sessions with RSVP. I have completed two half-marathons and lost 10kg after putting weight on from being on anti-depressants. I never imagined I would take this deeply kept secret to court. I remember feeling like I wouldn't ever tell another person, never mind have the courage to tell the police.

My life has been turned upside down, the foundations shaken and crumbled and I am still experiencing the effects of sexual abuse. I still can't have a 'normal' sexual relationship. I never think about sex and it makes me feel very uncomfortable watching anything sex related on TV. I can see how far I've come on this road but I also know I've got a long way to go. I'm finding everything difficult to deal with right now – I feel overwhelmed and I'm scared of having another emotional breakdown. I've always wanted to achieve a Master's degree, which I'm so close to achieving, but mentally I can't focus.

Tonight, I went through old family photos. I've wanted to look through photos to find some of myself as a child because maybe this will aid my memory. Maybe my inner child doesn't think I'm ready to know these memories? It is only through therapy that I've learnt that my adult self is disconnected from my inner child. I now recognise the importance of recon-necting but I'm scared of what this will bring. Will my inner child be angry at me? I need to be strong for her – she's been left alone since that time with no one to care for her, love her, save her and believe her. Since Steph died, I've become aware of my inner child – I think it's because Steph was such a mother figure and I miss her nurturing nature.

Whilst looking at old photos, I came across ones that hit deeply – I found one with me with 'him'. I still struggle to say his name. It shocked me because I wasn't expecting to see myself in a photo with him and also because I look so young. I've struggled to imagine myself at that age (11-13) and seeing the photo took me back to how I felt then – lonely and desolate of any love. However, seeing the photos have helped me feel able to begin the reconnection to my inner child – she deserves and needs the love she didn't get then. Therapy is coming to an end again – I wish this was the last time but I know I have so much more work to do. When will this end? It feels endless. I will keep showing up for her.

~ Sexual abuse isn't an experience of the past, it's trauma of the present until it is healed. ~

So, where am I now? I'm here writing about my experience in the hope that I can carry on the domino effect that helped me: one person sharing their story that sparks something within another to speak their truth and start to heal. I am a registered midwife and a certified neuro-linguistic practitioner (NLP) and emotional well-being coach. I have a deep passion to help others, to hold space for where they are and create space for their own growth and transformation.

I'm still on this journey of healing – it's a daily practice of honouring my needs, emotions and the continual processing of how those life-defining events affected me. What is different now is that the events that caused so much trauma and pain no longer have power to trigger a strong reaction within me. If I could change what happened, of course I would. But knowing that I can't, I choose to turn it into a positive – and that positive for me is a passion to help others find their voice and their peace. I used to think about who I would be if this hadn't happened to me but there are limitless potential paths I could be on. Yet one thing I know is I wouldn't be who I am today, and I am proud of who I have become and what I have achieved despite adversity. I believe in the human spirit to be able to overcome adversity and challenges; we don't grow when life is good, we grow because of overcoming the challenges. What often holds us back are the limiting beliefs we hold about ourselves and our ability to imagine what is possible for our lives.

'Love yourself through it.'
Lalah Delia

Things I wish I had known when I began
this journey...

One thing that I needed to hear often was that I could rest when I needed to – I am a very determined (and at times stubborn) person, sometimes to the detriment of myself. I want to remind you that during healing, you don't need to feel your feelings *all of the time*. It's okay if you need a break from feeling it all; taking a break is needed at times to integrate the work you've done so far. You might need to give yourself permission to tune out/log out/zone out and it is good to when it's feeling overwhelming. It isn't a race, there is no competition. This is your process so take it at a pace that feels right for you. This is a way that you can take back control. Being in connection with your feelings actually means noticing when you don't have capacity to be with those feelings right now. It is also self-care and so necessary during this process. However, it is important to notice the difference between needing to take a break versus avoiding feeling the feelings. The former is intentional with your own wellbeing in mind whilst the latter is an avoidance response that does not support or serve you. Getting to know this difference and noticing when avoidance tactics are creeping up is part of the learning to self-nurture.

....

BE PATIENT

Be kind to yourself – put down your weapons, this is
hard enough without you being hard on yourself.

Release expectations for what healing
will look/feel like.

It's okay (and important) to pause when you need to.

You can feel whole and complete AND broken and lost.

Not everyone will support you but
do it anyway for YOU.

Chapter 2

Healing the Mind

Dear little Stacie,

Wow, we have learned so much. The mind is a power-ful place that can either limit or liberate us. To go from our inner world and mind feeling like a prison to now feeling free from the suffering was once unimaginable. For so long, it felt impossible to be free of the mental prison. Although the abuse happened so long ago, it was affecting everything from relation-ships to feelings of depression and isolation. What I learned from going to therapy was the grief that I was carrying was so deeply buried. It took time for us to let it rise to the surface to let it out. It took 6 months of weekly sessions of tears for the grief to rise up and be felt.

I know the thoughts in your mind were telling you it was all your fault and you felt so full of shame and guilt but my journey has brought me to a place of understanding for why this happened – my darling, it was not your fault and I'm so sorry you carried that for so long. For many years, we were stuck in negative thought patterns that were highly self-critical and unkind. For those years we were also unaware of these thought patterns which kept us in that mental prison. We did the best with what we had and what we knew. It was a bloody good job that we kept going.

Fortunately, the healing journey signposted helpful tools that enabled us to see the negative patterns so that we could replace them with more positive and kinder ones. It is tricky when there's a crazy monkey jumping around in there but I know you know him well. Those thoughts and feelings were so heavy and hurtful.

Thank you for being so strong; you are one tough human and for that I will be forever grateful. I am in awe of your strength and resilience – our life could have gone in so many different directions and yet it was your grit and integrity that got us here today. I am so proud of you – of us. We survived so much and managed to get to point of being able to thrive again.

....

'Throw away the idea that healing
is forgetting, the real result is no longer reacting
to old triggers with the same intensity as before,
the memories are still there, but they do not have
the same power over your mind.'
~ Yung Pueblo ~

Sexual trauma has a neurobiological impact, i.e. it affects our brains and our nervous system. I am not an expert on the science and research of the wide-reaching effects of sexual trauma – I am only an expert in my own trauma experience. But what I would like to share here is what I've learned from my neuro-linguistic programming (NLP) training and becoming a therapeutic coach. By learning about how the mind works and delving deeper into the emotional wellbeing world, I have a more objective understanding about how my trauma affected my life.

I don't have many memories from childhood, even the happy ones. When people ask me what was good about my childhood, I look back blankly. This both saddens me but also frustrates me because after experiencing childhood trauma, I would love to be able to recall the positives of my childhood both before and after the traumatic events. My memories of the events themselves are limited, which was the reason why I thought it was impossible to report to the police. Fortunately, limited memories do not limit your ability to report abuse – how traumatic events affect the brain and memory are well documented and taken into consideration for historical cases.

My healing journey has unearthed insightful knowledge to better understand myself and the psychological and physiological response to trauma. I now understand that my vague memory was a coping mechanism known as 'dissociation'. It is when we leave our physical body, physically present but mentally absent. To others this might appear that we're disinterested but in fact, it is signposting that our overwhelmed nervous system is in shutdown and in protection mode. Dissociation is common after any trauma – whether physical or emotional – but is often overlooked because a lack of awareness of what someone is going through. It happens when our experiences are too emotionally overwhelming to cope and those around us aren't able to guide us through the stressful situation or deny our reality. Dissociation is essentially 'numb' mental/emotional mode but is extremely exhausting upon the body. Dr Nicole LePera (The Holistic Psychologist) talks a lot about dissociation and her own experience in her book *How to do the Work.* Getting back into the body is how we regain presence into our lives – this will be discussed more in the next chapter.

The Mind

Humans have basic instincts and needs to thrive – survival instincts (safety and security), to fit in and to be accepted. We all have a need to be loved, and therefore children seek acceptance and approval from their caregivers and peers. Children feel the same full range of emotions as adults do but don't have the life experience or the cognitive maturity to be able to understand what is happening and why, so they express themselves through their behaviour. Children therefore can't work out cause-and-effect relationships between themselves and events that happen to them. The child will usually interpret an event to mean they are not good enough as a person and create a limiting belief about themselves that gets carried for a long time.

The human brain has evolved over many billions of years and evolutionary psychology suggests our brain, although sophisticated in many ways, was wired for primitive times on Earth. There were only three choices during primitive times when we were faced with sabre tooth tigers in order to survive – fight, flight or freeze, which are all linked to neuro-chemical reactions. During stressful survival situations, our brain floods our bodies with stress hormones adrenaline and cortisol to enable us to respond physiologically to the situation – the sympathetic nervous system is engaged, meaning our cognitive focus narrows. Strong emotions beyond a certain point inhibit our ability to think rationally.

As both humans and society have evolved, we don't have to fight, run from or hide from tigers, but we do have other perceived threats and psychological distress causing trauma. The perceived part of this is important – I will come back to why it is important. During a stress/fear response, the part of the brain that controls decision making, emotional reactions and memory gets hijacked. This can be referred to as 'emotional hijacking' – when we are stuck in the primitive nominal thought process of 'protection mode'. This was useful when we were needing to protect ourselves from predators, however, not so useful with modern life stresses such as job interviews that provoke fear and anger. The sympathetic nervous response is actually counterproductive post event when we actually need to engage the para-sympathetic system to heal from the trauma. Our nervous system thinks the danger is here now, even if we are safe in the present moment. We need to rewire our nervous system and unconscious mind to know we are safe now.

These physiological responses happen automatically (subconsciously) and the resulting response can be labelled as stress, anxiety or perhaps fear, and our behaviour will seek to move us away from what our brain has decided is going to be a bad experience (based upon our past experience). After such a painful trauma, we are often mentally re-enacting trauma responses and can often take this as our 'normal' state of being or our personality. I've often wondered who I would be if I hadn't experienced this trauma. How would I act differently? Who would I be now?

Our mind and the thoughts it creates are powerful. More powerful than we even recognise. The brain is a beautiful masterpiece in human design, which I cannot claim to know the complex intricacies of. However, for the purpose of this chapter, I want to make you aware of the conscious and subconscious (also referred to as the unconscious) minds. The conscious mind is our thoughts, emotions, sensations and memories within our awareness at any given moment whilst the subconscious is outside of our awareness. Sigmund Freud famously referred to the parts of the mind with a metaphor of an iceberg – the conscious mind being what can be seen above sea level whilst the subconscious is what lies beneath. If you have ever seen a picture of an iceberg, you will notice what is meant by the phrase 'just tip of the iceberg'; most of the iceberg resides beneath the surface of sea level. It is also believed to be the case with the subconscious mind.

The subconscious mind is a huge memory bank with an unlimited capacity to permanently store our memories and life experiences. The subconscious memory recall is usually intact with the details of your experiences, whereas the conscious mind might not be able to recall the finer details, if any. This is certainly true when we experience trauma; our mind protects us by suppressing the memories to the deeper subconscious mind and out of reach of the conscious mind.

The primary function of the subconscious mind is to store and retrieve data and to carry out the commands of the conscious mind. The subconscious mind is like an unquestioning servant that works day and night to make our behaviour fit a pattern consistent with the emotion we attach to thoughts, hopes, dreams and beliefs. The subconscious mind grows either flowers or weeds in the garden of life, so whichever gets planted here is what materialises in our reality.

When we are unconscious, i.e., unaware of our thoughts, they become automatic just like our beating heart and our breathing. This habitual thought process is what can keep us stuck in the past or worrying about the future, especially if the thought patterns are negative.

There are three kinds of automatic thoughts:

- **Neutral thoughts** – 'I will go to the shops today for food.'

- **Positive thoughts** – 'I can do this really well.'

- **Negative thoughts** – 'I'm so stupid, people must be laughing about me.'

Automatic thoughts often reflect habitual repetitive patterns and can be about anything we have ever seen, heard, or learned. Obviously, though, negative automatic thoughts are the ones that can cause us emotional distress and keep us stuck in negative patterns. How often do we question the source of our thoughts? We are taking in so much information all day long, consciously but mainly subconsciously.

The metaphor of a reality tunnel is a great way to understand why we each perceive experiences differently and therefore how trauma affects us so uniquely. We each have our own filter upon the world which gives us our own unique thoughts, feelings and emotions for how we receive and perceive our reality (this theory was coined by Timothy Leary). Perception is the key to our unique differences in how we experience trauma and therefore how we heal from it. From the moment we are born, we are building our own filter of reality and this will depend upon many factors including our environment, our experiences and our upbringing, which is influenced by our parent's view of the world (influenced by their parenting). Our life reference/experience grows as we develop and learn new things and this is how we build our own reality tunnel; the bricks are our beliefs, dreams and fears about ourselves and also the world as we view it. The tunnel grows as we do and the 'state' of the tunnel will be affected by the beliefs held within the bricks – are there many limiting beliefs limiting our view of the world or are there few bricks in which we can see new horizons and possibilities for our future?

There is a strong interconnection and correlation between the quality of our thoughts and our emotions and vice versa. They are interconnected; however, they are separate and this is an important distinction to become aware of during a healing process. It is easy to confuse them, but 'thinking' and 'feeling' are different. We are not our thoughts or our emotions; they are a part of us that we can become aware of and release once we recognise the message they carry.

Nothing you feel is wrong; all our emotions are valid. They are messengers communicating to us the things that need our attention, and they signpost what we most value. Have you ever asked yourself what the purpose of your sadness/anger/resentment/grief is? It isn't something that we are taught (unless you had psychotherapist parents), but learning this single tool in my emotional-wellbeing coach training has totally changed how I greet my emotions.

For example, by looking at the intention or purpose behind an emotion, we are acknowledging that the emotion is present (important first step) and we are asking it what it needs us to know to move through it in a healthy and productive way. This is essentially emotional self-regulation. This was a revelation to me. I wish I had known about this earlier on in my healing journey; however, it helps me now when difficult emotions arise.

Resentment may be showing you where in the past a need was not met and where you are stuck. Shame or guilt may be showing you where you have some internalised beliefs that do not serve you.

When we experience trauma, we can unconsciously believe that we are not safe, causing repetitive physiological stress responses, or that we must disconnect from ourselves and our needs because we cannot trust ourselves and others.

Six common trauma responses (content from Dr Nicole LePera):

1. **Self-betrayal**: abandonment of yourself and your needs in order to be loved or wanted by another person.

2. **People-pleasing**: fear of saying no, avoidance of conflict, guilt or shame for wanting to do things just for you.

3. **Addiction**: using a substance or activity to avoid painful emotions/regulate the nervous system.

4. **Catastrophising**: seeing the world as a dangerous place where no-one has good intentions.

5. **Hypervigilance**: a survival-fear state being hyper-aware of their environment and how others perceive them.

6. **Dissociation**: when a person is physically present but not mentally or emotionally present. This can feel like being detached from reality.

These are common trauma responses and can often be misinterpreted and judged by others who are not aware of the impact of trauma. This is why it is true that we can never know what someone else has been through/is going through. Often, survivors of trauma portray that all is well, when in fact, they desperately need help internally, but may be embarrassed or ashamed to talk about their experience.

Thoughts – Emotions – Behaviour

Research has shown that on average humans have 6,200 thoughts a day and it is estimated 80% of them are negative and 95% are repetitive thoughts. Many of our behaviours, emotions, and responses are automatic, and keep our attention so engaged that we don't have any capacity left to notice when that thought, emotion or response happened. We end up responding before noticing the sensation or thought that stimulated a response. Once we are engaged in the response or reaction, the opportunity to notice and change the response is lost (think about the last time you shouted at your partner or child and then immediately regretted it).

How often do you notice your thoughts and their 'quality'? If your answer is 'not very often', then you're not alone. Our minds are wired to make us believe our thoughts are truth and they are who we are. To observe our thoughts is like watching the clouds pass in the sky and even on the rainiest days knowing the blue sky is always there beyond the clouds. The blue sky is the mind, the clouds are our thoughts.

~ The ability to become the observer of our mental 'stories' and resulting behaviour is a vital step in changing emotional reactions. ~

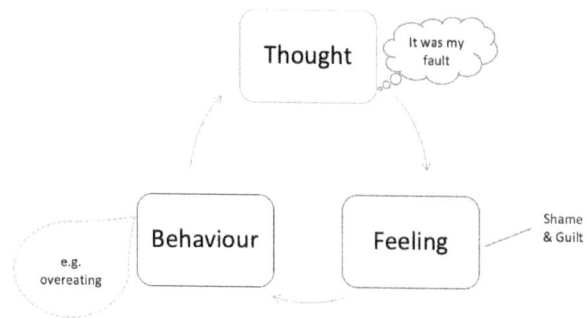

The diagram above shows how impactful our thoughts are upon our emotions and resulting behaviour. The mind likes familiarity so will thrive from going around in circles – we've all been there when we can't get out of a negative cycle of thinking/ruminating, and it is in this endless cycle that keeps us stuck from moving forward. This is done unconsciously, so this is not to create blame or for us to feel bad about ourselves; awareness creates choice. Once we recognise negative patterns, we can choose to interrupt the patterns and replace them with ones that make us feel better about ourselves to move forward. My understanding and knowledge of how the mind works and the effect our thoughts have upon our lives came from studying Neuro-Linguistic Programming (NLP), developed by Richard Bandler and John Grinder in the 1970s. In my quest to understand emotions and the mind, I became a certified NLP practitioner because it led me to want to help others to understand themselves and have greater control of how they feel, think and behave.

The reason I felt it was important to go into so much detail about the mind and the power of our thoughts is to highlight our unique and amazing ability as humans to self-heal through conscious awareness. The brain is neuroplastic, and it has the ability to form new connections to change and adapt the way it is wired based upon our experiences. Self-awareness really is a superpower, and so this is a reminder that choosing to self-heal and facing the inner darkness is worth the work. At the time of going through it all, it feels insurmountable, but with hindsight you will look back and appreciate your willingness to show up for yourself. Healing after sexual trauma involves the bravery to face the depths of trauma head-on in order to reach emotional self-regulation – the ability to respond to stress in a flexible and adaptive way, allowing the nervous system to return to reset. This in turn builds emotional resilience for future life experiences whereby we can be emotionally flexible to return to homeostasis, inner neutrality to be able to experience and process a wide range of emotional states.

Honouring Your Grief

Honouring the grief resulting from trauma is such a big part of the healing process. Grief is a natural response to loss; we lose so much after sexual trauma. Grief is what we usually associate with bereavement of a loved one but grief can be felt when we lose something we value or is important to us. Sexual trauma takes so much away from us – physically, emotionally, mentally and spiritually. Healing after sexual trauma is a form of bereavement, grieving for what was taken from you or for what you didn't receive.

Elizabeth Kübler-Ross, a psychiatrist, developed grief theory based upon her experience working with the terminally ill – this has been adopted and adapted for other forms of loss.

Dr Kübler-Ross's five stages of grief are:

1.   Denial – Disbelief (it didn't happen).

2.   Anger – This doesn't always manifest as rage; it could be masking other painful emotions.

3.   Bargaining – 'Maybe if I hadn't have done that, it wouldn't have happened to me.'

4.   Depression.

5. Acceptance – Not necessarily a happy or uplifting stage of grief. It doesn't mean you've moved past the grief or loss. It may mean, however, that you've accepted it happened and have come to understand what it means in your life now.

We are unique in what we experience and how we experience loss and grief. And again, healing isn't linear so the ways you may experience this process may look and feel different. Maybe like me, you experience the steps simultaneously and at times, get stuck at certain stages. It is all valid.

Can you see themes of grief through your own experience?

Write a letter to your grief – what do you need to tell it?

How can you honour what your grief is telling you – what did you lose that was important to you? What can you tell your grief to fully honour it?

Write about your anger, your disappointments, your rage, your loss, denial, depression, sadness ... whatever grief brings up for you – write through the heartache.

Pain unexpressed is often inflicted back upon ourselves, or we inflict it upon others unconsciously. Pain inflicted is pain held tightly – we deserve liberation from pain and grief by expressing it safely. We often put out calls for help in different forms, but one thing I've learnt is that we must respond to that call ourselves first. We have to help ourselves because this is a process of reconnecting to ourselves and feeling safe to do it. Ultimately, our own heed to the call is what our pain and grief needs to feel validated, felt and released.

You may not feel ready yet to let this come through – that is okay.

Know that there will be a time when you will be.

Once you feel it, release it with love. Don't keep holding onto it.

*'Some of us think holding on makes us strong
but sometimes it is letting go.'*
~ Hermann Hesse ~

The Inner Critic

Essentially, to notice the quality of our thoughts, we need to become the observer of our minds instead of identifying with the thoughts. It takes daily practice to really notice and observe the nature of our thoughts but by doing so we become more self-aware, and this creates more choice of how we want to respond to the stories/thoughts. Becoming the observer of our thoughts requires new neural pathways in the brain that act as a monitoring system so that you get the warning before the automatic response happens to choose how to respond.

I can hear the thoughts of your inner critic right now – telling you that you can't possibly get to a place beyond your current state and attain a life after sexual trauma. I hear this a lot from people just starting their healing journey – where you are now is where you are meant to be, and we all start in that place of feeling we've got so far to go. If your thoughts are kinder than these ones, I applaud your progress already. To be able to start the healing process, we have to want it and we have to believe it is possible.

I am encouraging you to follow your own healing path and be curious as to where it will lead you. Move past the fear that is telling you that you aren't brave enough, you aren't strong enough, it was all your fault, etc. The reason why I can speculate about the thoughts you are having is because I had them myself 10 years ago. My hope is that hearing my journey makes you question what is possible for your future. I know your future can be brighter than your mind leads you to believe.

Trauma cannot be quantifiably measured – it is a lived human experience that is unique to each person. Don't let anyone tell you how you 'should' feel or how you 'should' deal with it. Only you can know that, and no, you may not know that yet, but once you reconnect with yourself, knowing that you can trust yourself, the answers will come. Seek support – you do not and should not have to do this alone. Start where you feel comfortable to and go where it takes you – where it feels safe.

Healing means knowing in the present moment that you are safe, that past memories no longer trigger a stress response or keep you stuck in fear or repetitive traumatic memories. We can teach ourselves new ways of responding that are more reflective of our current reality. Trauma is not something anyone can 'just get over' or something that is long in the past – it is a lived experience that will keep on a loop until we are ready to process the pain, move it and release it. No one can tell you when you are ready to do this.

No matter your experience in the past, even if it happened yesterday, you deserve a life after the trauma. If you are stuck in that place and feeling unable to move forward, there is no judgement here – it took me many years and many attempts to find my inner courage to act and move forward. It cannot be underestimated how much inner strength and courage it takes to face the deep wounds resulting from sexual trauma, or any trauma, for that matter. For many years after my trauma ended, I was in denial and dissociated from it to be able to function within the world. I have respect for that me who did an exceptional job of wading through life with such deep wounds. For showing up for life and yes, even the times when I considered not being on this Earth anymore. The pain can be so overwhelming that self-sabotaging thoughts arise; I had a few times where I did consider suicide during the darkest of days. This is sadly not uncommon, and if you are reading this and it resonates, know that you are not alone but that I am so very glad you are reading these words. It is possible to face the wounds, to move beyond their grip and move forward with your life.

Changing the way we describe ourselves can cause huge shifts upon our perceptions of ourselves. For example, moving away from labelling and harsh judgements from the inner critic and moving towards mindful awareness, compassion and acceptance will change how you view yourself and the world around you.

Instead of 'I am depressed,' say 'I feel sad and notice my mood is low.'

Instead of 'I am insecure,' say 'I am working on my self-confidence.'

One tool that has drastically improved my ability to observe my thoughts is practising meditation and mindfulness. I was introduced to meditation many years ago when I started therapy in 2011. I started with 5 minutes a day but committed to do this for myself each day, but what I didn't expect to come from it was improved self-love. I hadn't even noticed that my thoughts were self-loathing and very self-critical until I began to take this time each day for myself.

Healing the Mind

Talking Therapy

I cannot write this section without giving credit and appreciation to those therapists who helped me get to this stage of writing a book about healing after sexual trauma. I wouldn't be here now if it wasn't for the caring and compassionate souls who do this work every day; they are super heroes in my view. I was very fortunate to live where there was free access to specialist sexual trauma talking therapy through a charity – Rape and Sexual Violence Project (RSVP) West Midlands. Sadly, this is not the case across the UK. I highly recommend seeking specialist sexual trauma support where possible so that the support is specific and tailored to this type of trauma. It is critical that therapy for trauma is dealt with in a sensitive and professional way to ensure that further trauma is not caused.

With access to the internet, researching local provision is now at the finger tips and you can have the details saved for when you feel ready to take the brave step of calling them. The charity 'Mind' has a useful resources page listing the national support services for survivors of sexual abuse which is a great place to start your search and from there you can search within your locality for further support.

There are many therapy modalities for which I am no expert but I encourage you to go with what feels right for you. Do your research and trust your instinct when talking to potential therapists – it is critical to your healing that you feel comfortable and trust the person with all that you will bring to your therapy.

It is *your* journey – hold it with the reverence that it deserves.

Meditation and Mindfulness

A big part of my healing has been learning to meditate and practising mindfulness. Meditation and mindfulness are practices that bring us into our bodies and into our parasympathetic nervous system state. The mind likes to ruminate about past and think ahead into the future about potential outcomes, keeping us either in the past or in the future. This usually results in being on autopilot in our day-to-day lives and not experiencing the here and now. In a way, this is also dissociation if we are not aware of our experiences physically, mentally, and emotionally. The key to healing after trauma is feeling safe enough to experience the feelings of the trauma in the present moment to be able to process and move through them.

Meditation and mindfulness are often synonymous because they both require awareness of the present moment. There are many different variations and ways to practice finding presence and awareness. That's the beauty of this tool, you can find one that suits you and make it your own; there is no wrong way. When beginning a meditation practice, it is common to get frustrated that you've noticed yourself drifting off into thought but the fact you've noticed you've drifted off is the act of meditation – noticing thoughts and bringing your attention back to the present moment is the point of it.

The mind mainly lives in the past, reliving memories or projecting into the future, deliberating all the possibilities, and both can be tiring. What this means is that we aren't paying attention (consciously) to our lives in this present moment.

I invite you to close your eyes for a moment and take a conscious inhale and exhale and ask yourself how you're doing in this moment. This is what being mindful of your present life is. How often do you do this? I'm not judging if your answer is 'rarely' or 'never' – I too need reminding to do this in my own life. The phrase 'monkey mind' is one way of describing our scattered thoughts. Our minds are programmed to run off, but we have the power to control it instead of it controlling us – imagine that!

Meditation and mindfulness have been practiced for many centuries in Eastern cultures and have become increasingly well known in the West for the health benefits. I think these terms can often have pre-conceived perceptions attached to them, but as with anything, we need to experience them for ourselves to have a true understanding of the benefits and how to best utilise them for our own benefit.

I encourage you to try guided meditations for beginners (there are many free and paid apps out there to choose from) initially – don't be disheartened or judge yourself for doing it 'wrong' – it is called a practice because it takes effort and commitment. Meditation is now one of my daily non-negotiable tools because of the benefits it brings to my mind and general wellbeing. There are other ways to meditate other than sitting, such as walking or creative activities like drawing, painting or colouring – you can be making yourself a cup of tea mindfully (noticing each step with awareness) and this is mindfulness/meditation. When you bring attention to what you are doing and with intention to be present, this is meditation.

Find what works for you to be in the present moment; know you are safe in this moment and in your body. The more you do this, even just a few minutes a day, the more you will learn the safety to be in your own body and presence.

Observing the Mind

Set yourself the intention for one day (or even an hour if a day feels too much) to observe your thoughts and notice any patterns/repetitive thoughts. This is the first step in being able to recognise the mental dialogue we have with ourselves.

Notice whether the thoughts are positive/negative towards yourself.
Notice the quality of them – are they self-critical or are they helpful?
Make note of the both the self-critical and helpful thoughts so that you can keep a track of the frequency and of the tone of you mind.

Honoring Your Emotions

An important way to reconnect to your feelings it to recognise what you actually feel. I
know from personal experience that initially,
after a long time of suppressing painful emotions, I felt numb and had no idea what I was
feeling. Talking with a therapist will support
you in this process of identifying and processing your emotions but there are also ways of
doing this yourself when you feel safe enough
to do some of this work on your own. Nothing
you feel is wrong, it just needs acknowledge-
ment and curiosity for what the message is
behind its presence.

Sit with the feeling without judgement – how
are you experiencing it?
Does it have a place in the body? Does it have a
colour or a sound?
Give the emotion a label that feels right for
you.
If you were to look beneath the emotion, what
is the need that wasn't met?
When you can identify the need, you can
honour it and tell yourself what you needed to
hear then.

Journal Prompts: The Mind

o   What are your thoughts telling you
     today?

o   Do your thoughts match how you feel?

o   Write down all the negative/hurtful
     things you've ever been told.

o   Then, draw a line through them all/rip
     the page out, and tear the page up/
     burn the page.

o   What are your hopes and dreams for
     your life?

o   What mental baggage are you carrying
     that you want to leave behind?

o   Today, my mind needs ...

.

Chapter 3

Healing the Body

Darling girl,

I am here with you. I love you. You are safe.

There is something important I want to talk to you about.

I feel it is important to share with you the learning that therapy and healing has brought. It took a long time to recognise the body shame that we felt. It is still a 'work in progress' but the biggest step was acknowledging that there was a distorted self-image as a result of what happened.

I remember feeling shocked that these men wanted to touch us when we were undeveloped in the chest/ breast area – we were bullied at school for being an 'ironing board'. This was double whammy cruelty. We hated that we weren't developing a feminine shape, and this created even more pain and misery. This took the body shame to a heightened and extreme level that impacted upon our future decisions for wanting cosmetic surgery.

It affected our sexual development and sexual experiences; we are still reclaiming our sexuality, and that is progress. The anger and sadness about this long-lasting effect is something I am still working through. It comes in waves. The difference is I now acknowledge these feelings and validate them. We were robbed of 'normal' sexual development – by 'normal' I mean the freedom to explore what feels good and to have boundaries when something feels wrong, without shame and guilt. Sex and sexual pleasure have felt 'bad' and 'wrong' throughout our life. How is that fair? The answer is – it isn't fair. Nothing was fair or just about what happened. It's good to allow ourselves to feel that and move through it to reclaim our power and body back.

I want to tell you that you are perfectly imperfect – what is most important is that you are a kind and caring human that always wanted to help others. You always had a smile for others even when you were hiding your own pain and sorrow. I'm not going to pretend that it doesn't matter about physical appearance because sadly, in this world it does, but not as much as you think it does. You are beautiful on the inside and outside. It has taken a long time to be able to say that, and yes, there are days this self-belief wanes; however, we are rich now because I have found our self-worth. These things aren't taught enough from a young age, and you couldn't understand these complex things at that age because you were still developing: physically, cognitively, and emotionally.

I know you held on tightly to body shame for so long, not knowing what it was, but I am here to free you from it. It was not your fault – none of it was. Our body has been reclaimed as ours again. It hasn't always been an intentional act to reconnect mind and body, but reflection upon the past decade has shown how necessary it was and how we are now on our way with this. Our mind and body are ours and they are sacred.

....

~ Learn how to listen to what your body
is telling you – it is your home.
Your body holds all the wounds and also
holds all the wisdom of how to heal them.
Listen for the wisdom. ~

This chapter will explore the impact that sexual trauma has upon the body and how we can reconnect to feel safe in our 'home': our body. The mind and body are connected, often referred to as the mind-body connection, and fundamentally this means that our thoughts, feelings, beliefs, and attitudes can positively or negatively affect our biological functioning. Our minds can affect the health of our body and the body's ill-health can affect mental wellbeing. There is overlap between this chapter and the previous (Chapter 2: Healing the Mind), and they could have been written as one, but I wanted them to be useful chapters within their own right. The Healing Toolkit sections again could have been written for either and both – once healing begins, you will see shifts within your inner and outer realities.

Sexual trauma can make your body a difficult place to live, physically and mentally. Sexual abuse affects us in every way, mind, body and soul. It causes disconnection from self as a coping mechanism. It puts the brain and body into survival mode, also known as 'fight, flight, or freeze'. Whether it involves a shock trauma (a one-off incident) or developmental trauma (a series of incidents during childhood), the coping strategies typically involve disconnection from the mind and body for a period of time.

Sexual trauma is an extraordinarily stressful event that results in emotional and psychological trauma, affecting our sense of safety and security and putting the body and mind in the 'stress response' (fight or flight). It's not the objective circumstances that determine whether an event is traumatic, but your subjective emotional experience of the event. This is why each person's experience is so unique because each 'event' is different but also the individual's emotional response is unique too. Emotions generally are not relative; they are a combination of our past experiences, subjective perception and our nervous system's instinctive response. This is why all emotions and emotional responses are valid; they do not need to be qualified and should not be dismissed by you or others.

If sexual trauma occurs during childhood, it affects brain and social development; it interrupts the wiring from connection to protection. Humans are designed to be social beings, requiring connection to others whilst also needing safety and survival. The need for safety goes beyond just the physical such as shelter and food; we also need emotional safety and warmth. Developmental trauma affects the usual wiring, changing the way the brain develops and causing disruption in the part of the brain that influences and controls self-regulation. Fortunately, humans and the human brain are highly resilient and have the capacity to self-heal and repair. The reason for detailing the developmental affects and the neuroscience behind childhood trauma is to give you permission to be where you are and to know change and healing is possible. It was not your fault. Ever.

Psychological trauma can leave us struggling with painful emotions and memories, and it can create anxiety that puts the mind and body on constant heightened alert. There are a wide range of psychological effects that are not limited to feeling guilt, shame, numb, disconnected, and unable to trust other people and even ourselves. There is no 'right' or 'wrong' way to think, feel, or respond, so it's important to give yourself permission to be exactly as you are. Your responses are normal reactions to abnormal (and abhorrent) events. Removing judgement of self is so important during the healing process.

It is common that trauma survivors do not have clear memories of their trauma but do experience symptoms that indicate what they've been through. These symptoms and effects of trauma will be experienced even when a person has no recollection of trauma. The effects upon a person and their life represent how the person coped or adapted to what they went through. For example, feeling numb or switched off emotionally is a coping mechanism to prevent the person feeling pain and therefore serves a purpose as an emotional anaesthetic. For some, memories do not return until many years later and can make a person question their reality and even their own mental state.

Common symptoms survivors experience (this list is not all the possibilities but gives an idea of what can be experienced):

Depression
Anxiety
Nightmares/flashbacks
Self-harm
Substance abuse and/or eating disorders
Difficulty sleeping
Shame/worthlessness
Chronic pain/illness
Hypervigilance
Panic attacks
Lost sense of self
Poor concentration/disinterest
Feeling numb
Dissociation – 'out of body'

When the trauma is a past event but the symptoms and effects persist, they are no longer serving us. These coping mechanisms may negatively impact upon quality of life and relationships. Unresolved/ unprocessed trauma manifests within the physical body. The body holds and stores all of our experiences, even when the brain is in protection mode and limiting the memories of the trauma. Trauma can get stuck within the body until it is moved and processed. Research is unequivocal that unresolved trauma results in disease and results in shorter life spans. The combination of disconnection from the body and the self is what makes it difficult to inhabit the body on a mental level. Stress is more than a mental state – it affects our whole being and creates disharmony. This is why I knew I needed to write a book about healing the whole self, mind, body and soul. One cannot exist without the other – there is no wellbeing without all parts of ourselves.

At university, I became aware of abdominal pain that worsened during times of stress, but there was always this underlying level of discomfort. I've lived with this for many years, and it wasn't until recent years and after many medical investigations that I got a definitive diagnosis of irritable bowel syndrome (IBS). I've come to learn that IBS is quite typical after experiencing trauma. Trauma manifests within the body in many ways, usually to get our attention, but we aren't programmed to tune into the body as a way to tune into ourselves and the messages that the body is trying to tell us.

A book I highly recommend to find out more about the body holding trauma is *The Body Keeps the Score: Mind, Brain and Body in the Transformation of Trauma* (Bessel van der Kolk, 2015). Dr van der Kolk in his book talks about how when animals experience trauma, they naturally shake to release the tension and to process the experience; they literally shake their body. Humans don't seem to have that intuitive connection to the body as a way to heal, and this contributes to trauma getting stuck and having a long-lasting effect and impact.

The reconnection to the body requires learning to feel safe and comfortable within the body again. To do so, we need to move from a heightened nervous state (sympathetic nervous system of 'fight, flight, or freeze') to the parasympathetic nervous system 'rest and digest' state. In this state, the body relaxes, our heart rate and blood pressure fall and our digestive organs are much more functional; this is the state that our bodies can function best in. The mind and body need assurance they are safe to move from a state of alarm and hypervigilance to a state of calm and presence in this moment.

> *'Neuroscience research shows that the only way we can change the way we feel is by becoming aware of our inner experience and learning to befriend what is going on inside ourselves.'*
> ~ Bessel A. van der Kolk ~

Sexual Healing: Reclaiming Your Power

This is still an area of my life that I am reclaiming. I'm learning what it means to be sexual and what sex and pleasure mean to me. I didn't know what it meant to feel safe during sex and what sexual pleasure even was. There is no 'normal' when it comes to sexual expression but one thing the trauma made me feel is that I wasn't 'normal'. It made me feel inadequate and 'dirty', even though I did not consent or choose what happened. Initially in my healing, there was a lot of anger around that, but now I choose to see that I have a choice for my future and I refuse to let it continue to have the power over me. I am worthy of pleasurable intimacy with my husband. When I started therapy in 2011, I needed space away from sex and intimacy, and this was because I was feeling the suppressed raw emotions of the trauma and adding this was too triggering. It felt like I had to clear the slate and begin again, but on my terms. For me, that looked like not having sex for a few years, but that's what I needed to do to care for myself during those years of deep inner healing.

The reason why this chapter comes after 'Healing the Mind' is because to feel safe enough to explore our sexuality and reclaim that from our past, we must move from the protection mode of the sympathetic nervous system to the safety of the parasympathetic nervous state. To heal sexually means to anchor safety in the mind and body. Our nervous system must feel safe. Not having a sense of safety in the body can lead to many issues sexually: shame, pain during sex, repeated unhealthy relationships, numbness and shutdown, to name a few. In my early years of sexual experiences, I dissociated from my body and mind in order to just 'get through'. It was a robotic act that rarely resulted in self-pleasure. Dissociation is when you remove yourself from the here and now in order to protect yourself from further harm and trauma.

This chapter has probably been one of the hardest to write. The reason is because I can't talk about healing the body without talking about sex and intimacy.

This is an area of my life I am still working through. My first sexual experience was abusive and traumatic. This filtered into every sexual experience consequently. I feel that my trauma robbed me of healthy sexual development. Of course, there is a difference between sexual trauma happening in childhood versus adulthood in view of brain development, however, it is also dependent upon the age of the child (the stage of their brain development). There's no wonder I felt anxiety rise up in me writing this chapter but I am committed to being a voice where there is silence and shine light where there is darkness. This is that place and here is my vulnerability.

I have no shame in saying this is an area of my life that still requires my love, tenderness and compassion. There were times when I felt completely and utterly enraged that this was taken from me – to experience sex in the way that it was designed for us as humans. To experience connection and love. Connection and love in the same sentence as 'sex' did not exist for me. Not until a few years ago, when I found a loving and supportive partner who loves me so deeply that I feel safe enough to explore pleasure and sex and what they mean to me and ultimately, what I want them to mean. I recognise that this is healing 'in progress', but I have learned how to build up trust and safety being in my own body and within the healing process itself, gaining more pleasure than I have ever been able to experience before. This is progress and this is what being 'in' the healing process looks like.

Sexual trauma impacts the person's sex life differently. You can experience both extremes – not wanting sex at all to hyper-sexual activity. I have been on both ends of the spectrum, however, when I engaged in sexual activity in my younger years, I can now reflect that I was totally disconnected from my body. I was disconnected from my emotions and actually felt numb to any sensation or emotion. I now understand that this was a protective strategy and the act of sex was ironically a cry for connection and love. I didn't know how to 'do' sex or how to feel but it made me feel unsafe and uncomfortable. I engaged in sex in the 'freeze' brain mode, just to be able to get through. I can also reflect back upon teenage experiences and see that these contributed to my already existing trauma despite them being consensual. The reality is, after such a traumatic experience, we can put ourselves in retraumatising situations because they are familiar to us. This is not to say that we do it consciously – the brain makes connections to the ones previously made and they feel familiar and therefore the connection subconsciously is 'safe'.

When we get to a point in our healing that we can recognise these scenarios, it is important that we don't judge ourselves for what we did or didn't do. We were doing the best we could with what we knew and with the emotional resources we had at the time. Once we know better, we can choose better. Healing is recognising that you deserve better and taking steps towards that.

'Forgive yourself for not knowing
what you didn't know before you learned it.'
~ Maya Angelou ~

Our body is our home in this life; we can't escape it so how we feel about it will impact us mentally. By improving our relationship with our body, we can improve our overall sense of wellbeing to the quality of our thoughts and body image. My relationship with my body is a work in progress. I am a lot less critical than I used to be but I do go through cycles of being hyper-critical versus somewhat accepting of it. To be able to build a better relationship with my body, I first had to become aware of the mental dialogue and catch it in the act.

It is only in recent years, that I have really recognised my disconnection from my body and sexuality/sensuality. My reconnection to my emotions came first through talking therapy, but I was slower to recognise that the mind and body were interlinked and connected in ways that I am now exploring in detail as part of my own healing. This is why I say that healing looks different for each person, as it should because one size certainly does not fit all. We all need different things to heal, and what we want from healing will be different and unique to us.

It was through mindfulness practice that I began to build a relationship with my body, learning what its signals meant for me. Through movement, I have learned what feels good and what feels challenging for me. It has helped me be kinder and more compassionate for what it can and can't do. I now know that it was not my body that let me down during the times of sexual abuse. None of it was ever my fault. My body is my physical vessel to experience life and it does so much for me – my eyes give me the gift of sight, ears the gift of hearing and my feet carry me where I want to go. I have learned to greet my body with gratitude. It isn't easy after many years of being on auto-pilot but the healing process is about practice and patience.

Healing as a process is not a one-time event; it requires patience and repetition to break down deep wounded patterns. As I have mentioned before, healing isn't linear, so there is no manual to follow to attain 'healed' status. That's because we are all unique, and therefore, what we need to heal will be unique. I do not consider myself to be 'healed'; I am 'healing in progress' but what I do celebrate is how far I have come in loving myself enough to be here now. What I describe in this book is what worked for me but I encourage you to tune into what feels right for you and what your needs are.

It's okay to be a work in progress.
It's okay to have good and bad days.
It's okay to pause when you need to.
Allowing ourselves to be exactly
where we are is self-care.

Pregnancy, Birth and Parenting

As a midwife of 14 years, I want to honour how challenging pregnancy, birth and parenting can be as a survivor of sexual trauma. I myself have not yet become a biological mother, but as a midwife who has cared for sexual trauma survivors, I feel it is important to highlight the importance of this transition and the challenges survivors can face. For a survivor who embarks on the birthing journey, this can be a time of trauma triggers, physically, mentally, emotionally, and spiritually. Pregnancy and birth in themselves are huge transitional and transformational phases for pregnant people. This topic also demonstrates the interconnectedness of mind and body on a grand scale. Not only does a birthing parent have their own physical and mental wellbeing to think about, they also have that of their unborn child to consider and how their experience of sexual trauma will impact them both.

The Survivors Trust (UK) has a resource page designated to this topic of pregnancy and birth for childhood sexual abuse (CSA) survivors and an online resource www.thesurvivorstrust.org/pbpaftercsa, published in June 2019. The resource shares real-life experiences of pregnancy, birth and parenthood created through the collaboration of female CSA survivors, midwives and researchers. A respected and inspirational midwifery colleague and fellow survivor of abuse, Kathryn Gutteridge was part of this project and has also dedicated so much of her career to helping pregnant survivors. Kathryn set up the Hope Clinic in the Midlands, a referral centre to support maternal mental wellbeing and has also founded 'Sanctum Midwives'; an organisation that educates, represents and challenges stigma around sexual abuse and its impact during motherhood.

I know from talking to other female survivors who are parents that they worry about their children's awareness of sex, consent, safety and the ability to voice concerns surrounding this topic. The worry is that as someone who is sensitive to sexual exploitation, abuse and trauma that this may impact their children negatively, causing 'hyper-awareness'/anxiety for them. This is a topic that I think we need to have in society more openly to unearth what is a healthy level of awareness; one thing I do feel strongly about is that there needs to be more awareness and open dialogue about sexual abuse so that there is zero-tolerance for a culture of secrecy and shame to the detriment of survivors. In order to challenge and break down societal norms and 'taboos', we need to be brave enough to speak up and talk about emotionally difficult topics to shine light upon them.

Moving Trauma Through the Body

If trauma is stored in the body, then healing involves moving the body as part of the healing process. It means we need to tune into the body and its sensations to learn how it is communicating with us (it is always) – to listen to it and to give it what it needs. Mobilising the body is to mobilise trauma.

I have moved my body in various ways over the years of my healing. Running was my first love and I'm proud to say I ran two half-marathons during my therapy years. I ran to fundraise money for RSVP West Midlands, which gave me a huge sense of purpose in giving back to the charity that was so pivotal to me on my healing journey. One type of movement that has been particularly helpful in becoming aware of the mind-body connection is yoga – it has enabled me to have appreciation for what my body can do and does for me daily. What I love about yoga is that there are different types depending on what you need that day – I love vinyasa yoga for the days I need more energetic movement to move energy through my body but also love restorative yin yoga for the days when my body needs to slow down and actively rest. Yoga promotes mindful movement of energy and breath to guide you back into the present moment, out of the mind and into the body. As I have explored movement and what feels good for me, this now varies depending on what I need on a given day: running, yoga, walking and weight training. Some days, I need rest and that's okay too.

There are several ways we can access trauma held in the body to move and process it; symptoms and effects of trauma gradually reduce as we process our experience. Movement and awareness of the body are fundamental to this process; trauma disrupts the body's natural equilibrium, freezing it in a state of hyperalert and fear. As well as burning off adrenaline and releasing endorphins, exercise and movement can actually help repair the nervous system.

Ways we can move trauma in and out of the body:

- Moving your body regularly in a way that feels good for you – exercise should not be punishment for what you ate or for how you look. What exercise do you most enjoy? It doesn't have to be exercise you think you 'should' do, such as running and going to the gym. It could be dancing, yoga, boxing or martial arts. Finding the type of movement that you enjoy is a way of beginning the reconnection to self. Doing the movement of your choice is the way to move and process trauma.

- Somatic therapy – this is a form of body-centred therapy that focuses on the connection of mind and body using physical and psychotherapy for holistic healing. It helps the person to focus on the sensations in the body rather than the thoughts and emotions of the traumatic event. The physical focus is a way to be in the present moment and to learn to self-regulate emotionally whilst releasing trauma related energy. There are somatic therapists that can guide you through this modality if you need or want support.

- Mindfulness – whilst moving your body, bring your awareness to how it feels as you move, the sensations, your breathing and particularly notice the difference to how you feel before and after the movement.

- Consciously looking after your physical health – do you nourish or punish your body with food?

- Giving yourself permission to rest physically when you need it – being able to recognise when your body needs rest is a skill and the first step in being able to give it to yourself.

- Getting enough sleep – healing trauma is mentally, physically and emotionally draining. A lack of sleep also affects the quality of your thoughts and so getting into a regular and consistent sleep routine will allow your mind and body to rest, giving you the space to process what you need to.

- Notice the mental dialogue you have about your body. Can you create a kinder dialogue if it is on a critical loop? This can be hard initially and finding a kinder dialogue can take time, so being able to notice the dialogue is the first step in creating a kinder mindset.

Mindful Breathing

Breathing is an autonomic process of the body, i.e., we don't consciously control it, but actually, when we do, it has many benefits. There is lots of research on the benefits of mindful breathing, also known as 'breathwork'. Breathwork has become known and practised as a healing modality in itself and I have incorporated it into my own healing toolkit in the past few years. Consciously changing the breath activates the parasympathetic nervous system which is the state we are aiming to access when wanting to heal after trauma.

There is no right or wrong way to breathe, however, the point of it is to do it mindfully to bring our awareness to the breath and the body. Start with 5 minutes each day where you sit comfortably where you won't be disturbed and focus on the in-breath for 4 seconds and prolong the out-breath for 6-8 seconds. The idea is that the exhale is longer than the inhale, which has a calming effect upon blood pressure and the nervous system. You can find a rhythm that is comfortable for you – some people like a longer inhale/exhale duration so experiment and find what works best for you. As with any of these suggested exercises, do what feels good for you. This is your healing and that means identifying what helps and leaving out what doesn't.

Try this exercise each day for a week or even two, and take note of the differences that you notice to your sense of wellbeing.

Journal Prompts: Healing the Body

Write a letter to your body telling it how you feel about it – it could be letter of apology or a letter of gratitude. Be honest but also try to bring compassion and forgiveness for how you feel.

- What is your relationship with your body like?

- What does your body need today? Can you give it what it needs today or this week?

- What is the mental dialogue like towards your body?

- How can you be kinder to your body today?

- How does your body feel today?

- What would it feel like to feel safe and loved in your own body?

○ Can you identify where you hold trauma in your body? It can be felt as sensations or tension in times of stress.

○ Write down the parts of your body that you love.

○ What does your body do for you that you can be grateful for?

Chapter 4

Healing the Soul

~ Healing the mind leads to
healing of the body.
Mind-body healing leads to
healing of the soul. ~

To the brave girl who got me here,

*What a journey we have been on so far in the last 10
years. We continue to heal; I will continue to keep
putting us first. I couldn't be here now if it wasn't for
reconnecting to you – my inner warrior. A big part of
reconnecting to you was getting to know you again
which was made possible when I felt safe again,
releasing the fear, guilt and shame. This healing journey has taken me on an exploration of your beautiful
spirit and soul, who we are at our core essence. It
wasn't easy at first because our mind had shut off
memories of childhood to protect us from the bad stuff*

but that also meant it shut out the good stuff accidentally. It took time and patience to seek the answers to who we were at our core.

Thank you for trusting me again and showing me what you, my inner child, loved doing and what brought me joy. Joy is not a word I had felt – it was unfamiliar and so we had to explore and seek out what did bring us joy. What happened to us is not who we are. We love singing and dancing, roller skating, going on bike rides in the sun, walking in nature, creativity for self-expression, writing surprise notes to loved ones, handwriting and so much more. Getting to know you has been one of the best things I have done in my life ... it is you, me, we and I. To know oneself fully – the light and the dark – is the only way to achieve peace and happiness.

You, my darling warrior, are strong, resilient, caring and deeply loving. You are my brightest light that got me through the darkest of days and shadows. Reconnecting to you, to our whole self has been the best thing to come from all the dark things that happened. We couldn't control what happened but we made the decision to control what we did with the after effects.

....

~ Courage is not the absence of fear
– it is taking action despite the fear. ~

It wasn't until I started writing this book and think-ing about my healing journey that I made the connec-tion that to heal and to feel wholesome, we must nur-ture our spirit/soul. Use what word resonates most with you. I interchangeably use these words. Even without my conscious awareness, this process was happening through reconnecting with my inner child. We are not the societal labels that we are given such as daughter, wife, mother, friend, sexual abuse victim and even 'survivor'. We are so much more than these. Take away these labels and who are you left with?

In essence, the spirit/soul is who we are at our essence, when you take away the labels, when you take away the trauma. Who are we if we don't iden-tify with our thoughts, our body and our emotions? This isn't always a clear answer because we may not have ever asked ourselves this before. This was a big turning point for me in my healing because I had left my inner child behind, and I had abandoned myself in trying to cope with the pain and darkness inside. I bring kindness to this now because I understand that I was doing the best I could at the time – I was surviving. Since reconnecting with my spirit, I've gone from surviving to thriving. To enjoying being in my skin, feeling safe to feel my emotions and knowing that I can trust myself again. I can still be my own worst critic and I still have emotionally dark days – I am human, after all – but the difference is that I can now show myself kindness and compassion. It takes practice and dedication after so long living deep within the self-loathing place. I can now recognise I am worthy of this love, love for myself and love from others. My wish for you is that one day you also believe this of yourself. If you already do, this makes me so happy.

Inner Child Reconnection

If the trauma you experienced happened in child-hood, as was the case with me, I encourage you to reconnect to your own inner child. The letters to my inner child that I have written throughout this book are one way that I have found to help me in this process. Inner child disconnection is essentially dis-connection from your inner world and a sense of who you are at your core, your essence. Dr Nicole LePera defines the inner child as 'an unconscious part of the mind in which we carry our unmet needs, our suppressed childhood emotions, our creativity, our intuition and our ability to play'.

When trauma happens in childhood, it is common that the memory suppresses memories of both positive and negative events. It isn't surprising that this happens when we try so hard to 'forget' what happened to enable us to get through life.

Trauma in childhood, when the brain is still developing, often leads to confusion about the complex emotions experienced. It can lead to feelings of loneliness, isolation, anger, and disconnection. As was discussed in Chapter 2, children don't usually have the vocabulary and life experience to express their emotions in an articulate way (dependent upon age), and so their behaviour reflects their inner world. This is compounded if care givers/parents do not listen, support and believe what children tell them and if the real purpose behind the behaviour is misunderstood. In NLP, we believe that 'all behaviour serves a purpose', and it matters whether the adults in the child's life are seeking that purpose for understanding or not.

The first and very important step of beginning a reconnection to your inner child is recognising they exist. If you struggle to imagine who she/he is, one thing I found helpful was finding photographs of myself when I was a child and using them as a way of seeing my inner child, making her more tangible. I have this one photograph in particular that is my favourite – I am aged 5 with a pretty dress on, standing proudly with a huge smile on my face. This was me when life was carefree, and all I knew was laughter and fun. I invite you to find the photograph that has this connection for you; it is powerful. You could put it up somewhere to remind you of your inner child.

There are several ways you can build a connection with your inner child, and as with anything during your journey, find what resonates with you. This could be sitting in silence, bringing your attention to your breath (mindfulness) and mentally asking your inner child to tell you what they want you to know. There are powerful guided meditations that you can do that help you reconnect too and are really helpful if you are particularly visual (I recommend the Insight Timer app). Of course, there is also writing letters to and from your inner child as I have used throughout this book. Later in this chapter in the Toolkit section, I suggest ways to start this writing practice.

A book I found helpful when I started this reconnection was a book that my therapist recommended: Rescuing the 'Inner Child': Therapy for Adults Sexually Abused as Children (Penny Parks, 2011) – it helped me to recognise the disconnection existed and how it happened. There are increasingly more books and resources that you can explore; inner child disconnection can happen for many reasons and this is now recognised within the realm of childhood trauma.

Intuition

What is intuition?

We all have our own inner guidance system; some call it gut instinct and some people call it their inner knowing – call it whatever resonates most for you. Our inner knowing tells us when something feels right for us or not, like our sixth sense. The reason why I am talking about this here in the soul/spirit chapter is because it is my hope at this stage that you can start to believe it is safe to trust your inner voice and your instincts. It was not your fault what happened to you – even when your inner critic has probably successfully convinced you otherwise. Your intuition led you to read this book. There is something inside of you yearning to believe that there is life after sexual trauma. It is safe to believe that now.

Trauma blocks self-trust and creates a disconnection from mind, body and often both. Self-trust and connection to the body are essential for us to be able to access our intuition. This is one reason why this chapter comes after mind and body – so that you can become aware of what needs healing for you, to be able to work towards building self-trust and a sense of safety, building a solid foundation for healing. Unprocessed trauma switches off intuition and self-trust. A reminder: it is a common effect of sexual trauma to question and doubt yourself and others because of a lack of trust. Self-doubt can lead to seeking reassurance, people-pleasing and co-dependent relationships, seeking answers or advice from others, which are all understandable when feeling unable to trust the self. I also find that there is a lack of education for children teaching us that we have intuition and therefore how to build a connection to it.

It is there within you – this is a process of undoing the effects of trauma bit by bit and rebuilding self-trust. It is there waiting to be accessed when you are ready. What word most resonates for your inner guidance to you? Throughout this book, I have been suggesting that you take what resonates and leave what doesn't; you have been using your inner guidance system whether you were aware of it or not. Use it as often as you can – it is your personal superpower.

For me, connecting back to my intuition has been the biggest gift of my healing journey. It was when I reconnected to my inner voice that I knew I had come so far along in my healing. That was when I knew I had called back the lost pieces to align my mind, body and soul. Intuition is a softer, subtle nudge, unlike the harsh and loud inner critic voice that is often quite demanding. Intuition is generally felt within the body – again a reminder of the mind-body connection that is so innate within us as humans. For me, when my intuition is telling me something is 'right' it feels expansive and good within my body. When it is telling me 'no', I feel a heaviness in my stomach. That heaviness in my stomach is how I felt pretty much most of my life up until my early thirties when I started to put the work into my own healing.

I can reflect back upon the last 10 years, and recognise the times when my intuition was trying to guide me. It was definitely guiding me several times before I acted to begin my healing journey. It wasn't the critical thoughts of guilt and shame – it was the loving voice that told me, 'Maybe I could get support so I can be free from the inner pain and sorrow.' Often, when we are ignoring our inner knowing, we can feel confused and might be thinking 'I don't know' when questioning what action to take; but I know when I'm thinking this – I do know, I'm just not listening. The intuitive nudges don't always make sense and can often feel scary to act upon but fear is usually a sign the action will take us out of our comfort zone and into personal growth. I don't mean fear when your body is trying to protect you from harm, I mean the fear of the unknown such as beginning therapy for healing, for example. Humans don't like the unknown; we want to be certain of an outcome so that we feel safe. Staying within our comfort zone restricts growth, so the next time you feel fear, ask yourself whether it is appropriately keeping you safe or whether it is keeping you from growth. You have the answers within you – it is time to start trusting yourself again and taking back your power.

I'm so glad I listened and followed the nudge to seek support because I wouldn't be here now writing this book and feeling free of the shadows of my past. I personally think that we all need to learn about our intuition as a child so that we know it exists and how to access it.

If you haven't considered a conscious connection to your inner knowing before, I invite you to close your eyes for a moment, take a few deep breaths in and out and notice how your body feels. After a few moments of bringing your attention to how you feel in this present moment, ask that your body shows you what a 'yes' feels like and then what a 'no' feels like.

Seven Steps to Accessing and Using Your Intuition

1. Be still – make time to close your eyes and sit in stillness each day, even for just a few minutes.

2. Tune into the body and focus on your breath for a few breath cycles. Notice how you feel. Notice where you are holding tension.

3. Discern the intuitive voice from mental chatter – the critic versus the softer, gentler voice.

4. Trust what the intuitive voice tells you.

5. Use the mind to find a solution/action for the intuitive guidance (the mind is the 'how').

6. Act on your intuitive nudge with self-belief and confidence.

7. Practice steps 1-6 as often as you can. This is a practice to develop a better relationship with yourself and the body's messages.

....

Diary Entry: Monday 19th September 2011

I'm not sure if there is a God but if there is, then my one prayer is to be happy in every sense. I don't need money – I just want inner happiness. Happiness seems to be elusive at the moment. I've cried so many tears I think I could have my own river. Maybe happiness is created from the inside out – maybe I can create and control it.

I think about my future a lot and what that will look like but I need to focus on today and not worry about what is to come – I can't change my past or know my future but I can control the here and now.

During the early days of my healing journey, I sought out meaning for what happened to me. I needed to believe there was a higher purpose for the trauma I suffered. This led me to explore religion as a way of finding faith and purpose. I was baptised as a Christian in 2012; the weekly visits to church were a solace for the inner turmoil I was experiencing, for which I am grateful. Now, I don't subscribe to one religion, I believe that all religions are pieces of the same pie and I don't personally need a label for what this is but, this belief is what brought me in touch with my spirituality; my spirit self. My spirituality is a gateway to reconnecting to self and the world around me – it gives me purpose and meaning to my life and my experiences. Now, if you're reading this and thinking 'What is she talking about?' that is absolutely fine, we all have our own belief systems and values. I encourage you to observe and even challenge your beliefs, especially if your trauma occurred when you were a child/teenager because your beliefs and values were formed during a time when you didn't know what was safe for you to believe. I don't necessarily mean challenge your religious beliefs (if you have them), I mean the negative ones that hold you back from seeing future possibilities for your life and your healing. The beauty is, we can always challenge our thoughts, beliefs and values and redefine them if we wish to.

The trauma took away your inner joy and emotional peace but the healing journey is a chance for you to call these back, piece by piece – ask your inner child how, they know what to do. You are your own healer. Allow your inner child to express themselves through play or creativity. What did you enjoy as a child – dancing, singing, music, drawing, writing? The point of self-expression is that it is unfiltered; it isn't supposed to be perfect or a masterpiece (maybe you find that you've suppressed your inner artist/creative). Maybe you feel called to write letters to the 'you' at the time the trauma happened to build that connection through writing. You can even write back from that 'you' to the 'you' now. The key is to not over think what comes out onto the page and trust what words flow across the page. If they don't flow at first, keep trying. It may feel unfamiliar at first but with patience and practice, a dialogue will flow and it will surprise you what insights come from it.

HEALING TOOLKIT

Healing the Soul

A common effect resulting from sexual trauma can be self-betrayal and self-denial because we don't feel worthy. The suggested exercises here are ways in which we can begin to reconnect – building self-worth and self-trust again. This section invites you to go on an inner exploration to rediscover who you are at your essence. Try to leave the inner critic aside as much as you can and set the intention to connect to your inner knowing – allow your inner child to take over.

**Reconnecting to Your Inner Child
Through Writing**

Firstly, how do you want to refer to your inner child? There is no right or wrong way to do this but it is important that it is in a loving and supportive way. You may find resistance comes up with this process and that is understandable but if needed, think about how you would have liked a caring adult to talk to you or how would you talk to a child (maybe your own now) that was upset/scared.

The aim is to begin communicating with your inner child to give them what they needed but maybe didn't receive back then. It is never too late to love, support and nurture this part of yourself and is the perfect way to develop self-love towards yourself. The aim is to also build a dialogue backwards and forwards to this younger 'you' and the 'you' now. This can also be done with your 'future' self and is a great way to open your mind to the possibilities of your future that may not seem possible yet.

1. Write a letter to the younger 'you' who may need love, support and nurturing – this can be the 'you' at the time of the trauma, or if that is too overwhelming, start with a time when you remember being upset as a child. Tell that younger self that you are an adult who will listen, believe and try to understand what is happening in their world. Write in language that feels understandable for the time you are relating to.

2. Write a reply from the little 'you' – how did they feel? What did they need? What didn't they understand then?

3. Repeat this process as often feels helpful. This may evolve over time as you do throughout the healing process so it is worth revisiting.

4. Remember, it's okay if it feels overwhelming; discern when you need to pause and come back to it versus when you're avoiding a necessary part of your journey. The intention is self-compassion for the younger 'you' but also for the 'you' now. Both versions deserve your love.

Healing Practice – What Do You Value?

From the list below, circle the words that stand out to you as what you most value (as many as you wish):

Acceptance	Calm	Competence
Accomplishment	Candour	Confidence
Accountability	Capable	Connection
Accuracy	Careful	Consciousness
Achievement	Caring	Consistency
Adaptability	Certainty	Contentment
Altruism	Challenge	Contribution
Ambition	Charity	Control
Assertiveness	Clarity	Co-operation
Attentive	Cleanliness	Courage
Awareness	Clever	Courtesy
Awe	Comfort	Creation
Balance	Communication	Creativity
Beauty	Community	Credibility
Bravery	Compassion	Curiosity

Decisiveness	Fidelity	Intelligence
Dedication	Focus	Intensity
Dependability	Foresight	Intuitive
Determination	Fortitude	Joy
Development	Freedom	Justice
Devotion	Friendship	Kindness
Dignity	Fun	Knowledge
Discipline	Generosity	Lawful
Discovery	Giving	Leadership
Drive	Goodness	Learning
Effectiveness	Grace	Liberty
Efficiency	Gratitude	Logic
Empathy	Greatness	Love
Empowerment	Growth	Loyalty
Endurance	Happiness	Mastery
Energy	Harmony	Maturity
Enjoyment	Health	Meaning
Enthusiasm	Healing	Moderation
Equality	Honesty	Motivation
Ethical	Honour	Openness
Excellence	Hope	Optimism
Experience	Humility	Order
Exploration	Humour	Organisation
Expression	Imagination	Originality
Faith	Improvement	Passion
Fairness	Independence	Patience
Family	Individuality	Peace
Famous	Innovation	Persistence
Fearless	Insightful	Playfulness
Feelings	Inspiring	Poise
Ferocious	Integrity	Potential

Power	Silence	Understanding
Present	Simplicity	Uniqueness
Productivity	Sincerity	Unity
Professionalism	Skill	Victory
Prosperity	Smart	Vision
Purpose	Solitude	Vitality
Quality	Spirit	Wealth
Realistic	Spirituality	Welcoming
Reason	Spontaneous	Wellbeing
Recognition	Stability	Wisdom
Recreation	Status	Wonder
Reflective	Strength	Worth
Religion	Structure	
Resilience	Success	
Respect	Support	
Responsibility	Surprise	
Restraint	Sustainability	
Reverence	Talent	
Risk	Teamwork	
Routine	Temperance	
Satisfaction	Thankful	
Security	Thorough	
Self-reliance	Thoughtful	
Selfless	Timeliness	
Self-care	Tolerance	
Self-love	Traditional	
Sensitivity	Tranquillity	
Serenity	Transparency	
Service	Trust	
Sharing	Trustworthy	
Significance	Truth	

Now, out of those you picked, choose 5 that are your highest values.

1.

2.

3.

4.

5.

Write next to the answers why these are important to you.

Now that you know what you value most, how can you incorporate these into your everyday life more? By making these a priority, you are reconnecting back to your core self and honouring your core values.

Healing Practice

Ask at least 3 people (more if you can) that you trust to give you the answers to these questions:

1. What do they most value about you?
2. What are your qualities and attributes they most admire?
3. What one thing could you change for your own benefit?
4. What is your greatest strength?

It may not feel easy to do this – typically, in British culture it is generally not etiquette to seek feedback/compliments about ourselves. If it feels uncomfortable, start with one person who you are the closest to and once you see the magic in the responses, seek more. The reason why this is such a powerful exercise is because others often see us in a very different light to what we see ourselves. Generally, we will see ourselves in a more negative light than what others do. By doing this, over time we can deconstruct the negative mental stories we have about ourselves and build more loving and supportive ones. This helps free ourselves of guilt, shame and mistrust.

Try not to disagree with their responses and convince them otherwise – try to accept their words with gratitude and love. Put these answers where you can see them often as a reminder of how others view you.

Ritual

A ritual is an intentional set of chosen activities that can be used to honour or release something. The word 'ritual' is steeped in religious dogma but fundamentally, a ritual is whatever you want it to be for what you want it for.

I have referred to intention a lot throughout this book – it is an important part of a healing process. Intention brings conscious awareness to what you intend to do. Attention and energy flows to what you put your focus upon. The intention of choosing your own healing is a conscious intent to put yourself first.

A suggested ritual to mark your intention to heal:

Light a candle, make your favourite hot drink and declare out loud your commitment/intention to your healing process. Write this intention down in your healing journal on the first page. This is a meaningful step in choosing yourself and wanting more for your life.

This is a suggested ritual but do what feels right for you. The aim is that it feels like a gift to yourself, no matter how small. Just making yourself your favourite hot drink with intention is a ritual in itself.

A Writing Ritual

A ritual that can be deeply healing is writing letters to those who have hurt you, where you say everything you have ever wanted to say to them and how they made you feel, and then burn them. Again, it is the intention behind what we do that creates the space for healing. As you watch the paper burn (safely), set the intention that you are releasing whatever you need to release, offer self-forgiveness and watch those words burn in the heat of the flames. It is metaphorical for letting go of what has hurt you and what may be holding you back. Make the ritual your own – maybe you do it alone or maybe you invite your support people to celebrate the release.

Do what feels good to you. This is permission to get creative in the ways that will empower you to move forwards to where you want to be in your life.

Practice Gratitude

This may sound simplistic, but there's definitely more evidence over recent years about the power of gratitude, which lies within its simplicity. Now, I do know from experience from the darker days of healing that gratitude is an elusive concept and it feels impossible to feel gratitude for anything – especially when you're being reminded of the trauma you should not have experienced. I hear you. There are days where it is necessary to fully accept how you feel in that moment. This is part of this process; however, the more you can be grateful for who you are, where you are and where you are going, the more light and hope can get through the dark cracks of desolation.

Don't just take my word for it: positive psychology research has shown that practising gratitude is strongly and consistently associated with inner happiness and wellbeing, building resilience to difficult situations and improving health. So, the more you can be grateful during the healing process, the greater this practice itself can help you through to better days.

There is always something we can find gratitude for, such as our home, our loved ones, food, clothes. But I would also encourage you to have gratitude for yourself for showing up for your healing. For showing up on the days where all you can do is get through the day – by sleeping, by crying, by screaming, by hiding under a duvet. Have gratitude for doing your best because yes, that is doing your best some days.

Daily Practice:

Using your journal, write down at least 3 things you are grateful for (bonus points for each extra thing you can write down). The more you do this, the easier it is to find things to be grateful for. You can do this any time of day; in the morning it's a great way to start your day, but equally, some people like to do it as part of a bedtime routine, ending on a positive note before sleep.

Consider how gratitude *feels* – the things you are grateful for make you feel the way you do for a reason. Do those things more often.

Journal Prompts

- Write down things you enjoyed doing as a child – what did you enjoy about those things? Do you still do them?

- What brings me joy/makes me feel happy?

- How often do you do these things?

- What makes me unique?

- What am I doing when I am feeling my best self?

- I am ...

- I am not ...

- I want to ...

- I want to stop ...

- Something new I want to try is ...

- One wish for my future self is ...

- My intuition is telling me ...

- I would regret not doing ... (think about your 80-year-old self and what they would regret not doing)

- What hopes and dreams do I have for the next chapter of my life?

- What would I do if there were no limits?

Chapter 5

Self-Love

~ The ultimate self-care is in choosing
your wellbeing and taking steps each day
towards how you want to feel. ~

Dear brave girl,

*This is probably one of the hardest letters to you. I
need to be honest and I hope you can forgive me. The
thing is, I neglected you and I have been unkind, even
hateful towards you. For so long, I didn't like what
was inside and this meant that I was self-loathing of
the person we are. I was so consumed by how the
abuse made us feel that I took that within and took
the hate out on us, the victim, the one who didn't
deserve any of it. None of it was our fault but yet the
irony is, it makes you feel that it is. It makes you feel
bad, dirty, unlovable, guilty and unwanted. I know
you know this – more than anyone – but I want to*

honour you in acknowledging it. I left you behind unconsciously because I was trying to leave behind what happened. I desperately wanted to get rid of the darkness, shame, guilt and sorrow that was inside but I now know that it isn't possible to bury trauma. We have to process it, move it and release it.

I'm sorry I didn't ever tell you that I love you. The one thing you needed then was love, care and belief and I could have at least given it to you. I'm not blaming myself for what I didn't know or understand then, but I am apologising for the fact you didn't get these fundamental needs met. You weren't supported by the adults in your life and this is why it is important I am here for you now. It has been so healing to learn I can give these things, this love, this care to us, to me. I am at least grateful that I learned about self-love through this journey and I commit to telling you/us regularly. Self-love is a practice and one I commit to every day. You deserve so much love and appreciation.

Thank you. Thank you. Thank you.

....

*~ Love yourself enough to know that
you can forgive yourself for your past;
it is not who you are. Choose you. ~*

I don't believe in coincidences; I believe in syn-chronicities. I am writing this section on self-love on Valentine's Day, which was not planned. In actual fact, I have had a day that has fully tested my self-love values and belief. I have had a mental conflict going on for a few days where my body is clearly telling me I need to rest but my inner critic is loudly protesting. My inner critic is telling me I don't have time to rest, I need to write this book, I need to clean the house, I need to ... I should do ... I must ... the list goes on. Then, I caught this very familiar thought pattern and paused. This pause gave me the space to remember the importance of self-care ... in this instance, giving myself a break and knowing that my ability to keep 'doing' does not equate my worth. This is what progress looks like – it isn't perfection; it's non-judgement and choosing differently.

It has taken me a long time to recognise that I am my own harshest critic, always pushing forward to attain something and then moving onto something else once that has been achieved. The reason it took so long to realise this was because I had to become the observer of my own mind and its thoughts to hear how I was talking to myself, about myself. It was a harsh reality to hear how much I berated, criticised and bullied myself because I wasn't meeting my own expectations. I had to take a deep look into this behaviour and reflect upon how I got to this place of complete self-loathing.

Shame and guilt. Two words that hold so much power and toxicity.

I remember the moment well when this 'toxic two' showed up and set up camp within me for so long. The moment I told myself, 'I was raped because it was my fault.' I was a bad person. Why didn't I stop it? How stupid I was because I allowed it to happen. I didn't know that we were meant to love ourselves; I wasn't taught 'self-love' and I hadn't seen it role-modelled to me. I can understand now how powerful the hold of shame and guilt had over me because, combined with a lack of self-worth and no awareness of self-love, my inner child didn't have strong foundations to build upon.

Our parenting is so important when building our belief foundations. If our parents were overwhelmed, emotionally unavailable, neglectful or abusive, then at a young age we learned that we were unworthy of having our needs met, which often leads to the conclusion that we are unlovable. Children observe and imitate how their caregivers practice self-love and self-respect. If parents do not model self-love and self-respect, how can we possibly know what it looks like for us? Our parents do the best that they can with what they know and have – if they were parented in unloving and neglectful homes, then this becomes their model of the world. Of course, there are exceptions and troubled children can learn in adulthood what self-love is and become committed to passing this learning onto their children. Sometimes, parents are carrying emotional pain and grief of their own and therefore don't have the capacity to hold space for their children when they're trying their best to get through the day to survive themselves. I'm not saying any of this to condone harmful behaviour from parents/care-givers, but I do bring compassion to the many humans walking the Earth that are wounded themselves. For some, the grief and pain are just too much, and so they continue through life suppressing and numbing, dissociating from their life and others.

It is my hope that one day it is taught to all children at school from a young age and that it is talked about throughout their education. It is a gift to possess self-awareness, to be conscious of our own thoughts, emotions and behaviours that not only impact ourselves, but also others.

I came across the terms 'self-love' and 'self-care' from my therapy. These were alien concepts, and even when I could cognitively understand them, it wasn't until I experienced what they meant to me that I able to integrate them into my life. This brings me back to my present-day example. Today, I took out my journal and I answered, 'What is my relationship to rest like?' This helped me to unpack my need to 'do' all the time and as always, it relates to a lack mindset and that I must be 'doing' to be able to prove my worth. This is what healing and self-care look like – being able to recognise the inner critic, observe without judgement and to greet it with kindness. Kindness and compassion are the antidotes to self-loathing and critique.

I believe self-care and love are a daily practice. Usually, it doesn't come naturally because we are conditioned to care for others and that self-care is selfish. I believe self-care is selfless – we can't give from an empty cup, so we must fill our own cup up full so that we can give so much more to others. There is a different feeling to the love we give when we truly love ourselves. Self-love, just like the healing process, cannot just be a thought; it must be felt and experienced. Self-love is, in essence, the uncompromising belief that we are worthy of love, respect, protection and belonging, regardless of our thoughts, feelings and reactions.

What Does Self-Love Mean to Me?

Being kind to myself – it means that I can catch my inner critic's thoughts, notice them and choose to think a kinder thought instead. The world can be full of harsh words and critique, and life can be challenging enough without our own self-critique. Put down your mental swords once in a while and notice how that feels. Do you believe all the negative thoughts about yourself without question?

Allowing myself to make mistakes – this is a big one for me as a self-confessed perfectionist. This one often catches me out but each time I do notice I'm hard on myself, it is a step closer to self-love. In reality, we need to make mistakes to learn and improve, so the fact we expect perfection to begin with is an unrealistic expectation.

My value is not based upon how my body looks –
again, this one is a tough one because I have battled
with body image issues, but I can recognise progress
now in that I show my body some compassion,
respect and gratitude. I am worthy, regardless of my
body and the changes it goes through. There are days
when the inner critic wins the battle but I am aware
of the thoughts and can at least notice they are
unkind.

Validating my own emotions and experiences –
releasing the old strategy of suppressing difficult
emotions. How I feel is valid and it is asking me to
acknowledge the messages my emotions are here to
tell me. I sit with how I'm feeling to acknowledge
what is present for me as opposed to dismissing it
because it's uncomfortable.

Giving my body sleep when it needs it – I often want
to get things done and get frustrated when my body
can't keep up with my 'to do' list. One thing I know
from 10 years of being on this journey so far is that
healing from trauma is tiring – mentally and physically. The best way I can care for myself when I feel
tired is to sleep and know that I need rest as part of
my healing.

Creating emotional boundaries – being able to recognise when others don't have my best interests at heart. A relationship should be mutually beneficial, whereby both people make the effort for each other.

I Love You, I Am Listening

Have you ever placed your hand on your heart, closed your eyes and said the words 'I love you'? Sarah Blondin guided this action in one of her meditations (search for her on the app 'Insight Timer') and the first time I did this, I cried with such sorrow. I was in my early thirties and realised I had never told myself that I love her. This brought me back to my inner child and how this meant I also hadn't ever told her that I love her.

Take a look at the quality of the relationships in your life – these will give you an indication of your inner world and how you feel about yourself. Our inner and outer worlds are often mirrors reflecting the other. I can reflect back now upon my relationships over the past 10 years since I've been on my healing journey, and the changes are beyond what I could have imagined. How I felt about myself in my early twenties was definitely reflected within my personal relationships – romantic but also friendships and familial ones. I chose romantic partners that reflected my low self-worth at the time, and as a result they showed me the level of respect and love that I showed myself. It's often that we can't see this about ourselves or our lives until we recognise and acknowledge by taking an honest look in the internal mirror. If we don't like how others are treating us, can we be honest about how we treat ourselves?

~ Make changes to your inner landscape and
your outer world will shift as a result. ~

It took me a long time to realise that I was allowing others to treat me badly because I didn't have enough self-worth to ask for respect from others. It is possible that my low self-worth was another effect of the trauma I experienced. However, I believe there are many factors that get interwoven with the complexities of self-worth and that the cause is less important than the necessity of improving it. Once I recognised that I was choosing unhealthy relationships and that I deserved more, I started making better choices for myself and learned how to implement boundaries within all my relationships. Emotional boundaries have been a game-changer in improving my self-worth because implementing them meant that I was saying, 'I am worthy of respect.'

Self-worth doesn't improve overnight; it takes a daily commitment to choose better for yourself. Even if you don't yet believe it yet, tell yourself you deserve more every day. This book is, in essence, the story of how I developed my self-worth through choosing better for myself. My hope is that you also see that you deserve more.

You deserve more love – for yourself and from others.

You deserve a life after sexual trauma.

Take an honest look at the relationships around you and ask yourself if these reflect your worth. What do these relationships mirror back to you about yourself?

One concept I have considered a lot during my healing is 'forgiveness'. My prior knowledge of this word was from my Christian education from attending a Catholic secondary school. I hadn't ever considered what it meant to me though, until one day I asked myself if I could ever forgive 'them'. What I have come to learn is that forgiveness is not about accepting and forgetting that it ever happened nor is it condoning or justifying actions that led to the trauma. Forgiveness is coming to a place of inner peace because how we feel about 'them' and what they did affects us, not them. On my quest to find out what forgiveness meant to me, I found out that it was myself that I needed to forgive the most.

# HEALING TOOLKIT

Self-Love

I know the word 'love' can be a strong word when you're just beginning healing after sexual trauma. The word 'love' is such a loaded word, full of concepts from romantic relationships, roses, intimacy and anything else that comes to mind when you read it. We all have our own filter on what the word means to us and so, this is my invitation to you to consider what this word means for you. How can we declare self-love when we don't consider what it means to us?

What Does 'Love' Mean to You?

What does it look or feel like to you?
How does it feel to be truly and deeply loved?
How do you/will you know you love yourself?

If the word 'love' is too much for you to use right now, consider replacing it with 'support'. I found this word easier to use practically as a way to understand what self-care was, how I can best support myself today and moving forward. What can I do to support my healing today?

As with anything in this book, I invite you to consider what is meaningful to you – replace any words that do not resonate. The intention is to start you on a self-inquiry, a journey that only you can take, but what's important is that you begin somewhere.

Ways to Love Yourself
Allow yourself to rest.
Forgive your past self.
Appreciate your body and what it does for you.
Choose yourself – what do you need most in this moment?
Preserve your energy for those that deserve it.
Protect and promote your inner peace.
Give space for your emotions – they are valid.
Listen to your inner child – what are they most needing from you?

Types of Self-Care
Physical: sleep, healthy food choices, rest, exercise, physical movement.

Emotional: space to witness and release emotions, self-kindness and compassion, self-forgiveness as a daily practice, journaling.

Social: support systems, boundaries, communication, quality time with those who deserve your energy, social media boundaries.

Spiritual: time alone, journaling, creating your sacred space, meditation and mindfulness, doing what brings you joy.

Work: breaks, work-life balance, doing work you enjoy.

Personal: hobbies, personal identity, honouring self, self-development.

Financial: money management, paying bills, treating yourself, saving, budgeting.

The best way to know if we are treating ourselves with love and respect is to notice how we are treating our bodies, our minds, our energy and our time.

Self-Care Practice: Self-Soothing
I encourage you to sit somewhere you won't be disturbed, close your eyes, place your hand on your heart and breathe. Notice how the touch alone feels. Tell yourself the things that you most need to hear – do you love yourself? Do you 'like' yourself? What are the kindest words you can say to yourself today?

Do this exercise as often as you can. If it is difficult initially, keep going. It will become a self-love tool on the days that you need it during your healing journey.

Imagine if we showed ourselves the same level of kindness and love that we offer to our best friend. Imagine how different it would feel to live in your own skin if you cared for yourself like you do your loved ones. Close your eyes for a moment and imagine how different it would feel – how different does it feel? Write it down in your journal so you can come back to this in the future.

Self-Care Practice: What I Most Need Today

Whilst on your healing journey, some days will be harder than others. Some will feel impossible, and then you get this random blue-sky day where hope pops through. Whatever the day, honour how you feel. Most often, there will be days when you just don't know how you feel – these are the days I encourage you to sit down with your journal and write at the top, 'Today, I feel …' and allow whatever comes up to flow out through the pen.

A way of tuning into what you need during your healing is asking yourself what you need today:

Is this a day that I need to attend to my mental/body/spirit wellbeing?

By asking this each day, we are breaking it down into manageable daily chunks – make a commitment to tending to those needs 'just for today'. This is a well-known saying/prayer from the 12-step Alcoholics/Narcotics Anonymous programme but I actually believe it is a powerful way to be more present in all of our lives, no matter the trauma we are healing from. Give yourself permission to provide yourself with what you need. It is okay if today you need to stay under the duvet and sleep – allow yourself to be exactly as you need to be without judgement. Yes, the 'without judgement' is probably the hardest part but if there's one thing I know from the past 10 years, it is that I could have been so much kinder to myself and what a difference that would have made. If you can't give it to yourself then take this as permission from me to you to be kinder to yourself, to be exactly how you need to be today.

Journal Prompts: Self-Love

Remember, write freely without filtering the answers and without judgement. Healing can only be invited in when we are honest about where we are right now. Your journal is a safe space and a place of non-judgement and acceptance.

○ Self-love is …

○ How would you rate your level of self-love, compassion, respect, and esteem out of 10? What may have led to these ratings?

○ Things I love about myself … (list at least 5 things or more if you can. Replace the word 'love' with 'like' if this feels too difficult to begin with).

○ One thing I find hard to love about myself is …

○ How can I love myself today? (make a commitment to do it today too)

○ I feel loved when …

○ What needs do I have that I find difficult to meet? What small steps can I take to meet these?

○ I feel safe when …

○ I feel supported when …

○ I feel comforted when I …

~ Self-love is in essence the uncompromising belief that we are worthy of love, respect, protection and belonging regardless of our thoughts, feelings and reactions. ~

Chapter 6

Supporting Healing

This journey is yours and yours only; however, we all need support. The effects of sexual trauma are far reaching; it doesn't just affect those who experienced it. It affects those who love us and therefore filters into their lives too, and for them to be able to best support you, they need space to feel how it affects them too. The aim of this chapter is to highlight the importance of support for you as the survivor whilst honouring the needs of those who support you. We all have needs during a healing journey and only we know what they are. One thing I believe is crucial to this process is open and honest communication. This isn't always easy, especially in the early days of this process, so be gentle with yourself and find the ways to communicate that are most supportive to you. Personally, I sometimes have to write down how I feel and share it with my loved one or send voice notes if words are too raw to express face-face initially.

I want to refer back to Chapter 2: 'Healing the Mind' here – it's useful to remember that we all have our own perceived reality, including the mental 'stories' of what others are thinking about us or what we think others are experiencing. This is why I can't emphasise enough the importance of open and honest verbal communication between survivor and supporter. We forget that humans can't mind-read, so it's important to consider each other by communicating what is your actual reality and experiences and vice versa. This process does require the survivor to understand that their trusted loved ones are not equipped with specialist skills, so understanding and recognising the support they are trying hard to give will go a long way in honouring their efforts.

Support can come from unexpected places. It doesn't have to be from the people we think 'should' support us. During the healing journey, people have fallen away from my life and I've also created new and nurturing relationships. What I found to be a turning point was when I recognised that I don't have to give my time and energy to those who do not deserve it. My healing brought me to a place of recognising my worth which meant that I began to create boundaries with people who did not have my best interests in mind, including disconnecting from them. Healing takes a lot of energy, and so protecting it for yourself is the first step in choosing what will benefit you the most and not doing what is expected of you.

Childhood sexual trauma that occurred either directly because of family members or involving them indirectly causes a lot of anguish for the survivor. I know conflict arises because of the knowing how morally wrong the behaviour is versus loyalty to them or other family members. Enmeshment is a term used to describe relationships where there are no boundaries and people are fused together by unhealthy emotions and behaviours, usually rooted in trauma.

So much guilt can come from these perceived loyalty ties and keep survivors silenced to protect the family. This is especially an issue for some cultures where this would bring 'dishonour' – this can be repeated re-trauma by keeping silent and putting other people's needs first. This is not judgement; this is a complicated factor that is part of some people's healing journey. Each journey looks different because of many factors, including the context of the trauma. however, this also may require healing. I have experienced fallout from others for creating boundaries within relationships from realising that to heal, I need to recognise my own needs including who/what is worthy of my time and energy.

Relationships in relation to healing after sexual abuse are complex, particularly if those relationships are interconnected to the abuse. There comes a time when we have to evaluate the benefit of these relationships (if any at all) on balance with our own well-being. One thing I have come to learn is we always have a choice, even when we can't always see that choice. I found this hugely challenging in the early days and it was often my therapist who would gently challenge these limiting beliefs – I now practice regularly the art (and challenge) of creating boundaries. This was a completely new concept to me and I don't know when I realised what they were and how to create them, but, in essence, a boundary is defining what you are comfortable with and how you want to be treated by others. Boundaries work both ways in a relationship, and we have to accept that we also have to honour the other person's boundaries, even when we don't agree.

Sexual abuse is one of the worst breaches of your personal boundaries that can happen; fundamentally, it is a breach of human rights (consent, trust and dignity, to name a few).

We often don't know what our boundaries are until they are crossed.

Examples of emotional boundaries include:

- Saying no when something does not align with your personal values or principles – or if you simply do not want to do something

- Expecting respect

- Being able to express your own feelings

- Refusing to accept blame or accepting responsibility for others actions

- Asking for and accepting help when you need it

- Asking for space/time alone

- Communicating your boundaries and needs

- Sticking up for yourself – know your own worth

- Your right to privacy

- The ability to change your mind

- The freedom to express sexual boundaries

- The ability to manage your own time

- The choice of when you want to feel vulnerable

- You always have choices/a choice

- Knowing when you need a break or rest

- Cutting contact with those who do not consider your best interests/one sided relationships.

I am incredibly grateful for those that have supported me to this day. There isn't a manual of how-to best support survivors because we are unique and each person needs something different. Thank you to those who didn't know how to support me but asked me what I most needed. Thank you to those who didn't support me. Thank you for showing me where I didn't have self-worth. You naturally fell out of my life because I realised my own worth; knowing that I deserved more and my healing was my priority, not pleasing you.

A Letter to the Supporters of Survivors Reading This ...

Thank you. Thank you for sticking around and showing your commitment to support. It is an emotional rollercoaster for all involved but thank you for trying even when you didn't (or maybe still don't) know how. Please keep trying even when you feel like you are failing. You are not failing because you are still here trying and that means a lot. Take care of your needs and how you feel – they are valid too. There are many healing tools suggested to help your survivor that I would also encourage you to do too – express yourself freely. Know that it is not your job to 'fix it' as much as you would like to; they aren't broken, and no one can 'fix' trauma. It is a process that we have to go through at our own pace, so honour your survivor's pace. If they are currently in a dark place, sit with them in the dark. Words aren't always necessary but knowing that you want to be there will help.

There may be times your survivor will unintentionally push you away (physically, emotionally, or both). Get to know when they need time alone but also when they need you there despite saying to go away. Sometimes, we emotionally test people by seeing if they will still will love us even when we feel unlovable and try to push them away. Try not to have expectations for how the healing process will be; no one can know this, it's experiential and unique to each person. There will be good and bad days; show your love and support through it all. This is hard for you too – take rest when you need to and be kind to yourself when you're finding it hard. Keep going – your support means the world to your loved one even if there are times they can't express it yet.

This is permission for you to not know what to say or what to do. No one is naturally equipped to support sexual abuse survivors through their healing unless you have received specialist training. The important thing is you want to support and to ask your loved one what they need. I think it's so important that, as a supporter, you are honest when you need your time to 'decompress' from doing the supporting, you have your emotional needs too. How you feel is valid, too.

....

A note to the survivor – your loved ones are trying their best, so remember to send them appreciation, whether it be a simple 'thank you', a cup of tea, a cuddle or whatever they would find most meaningful to them. If someone in your life is making you feel bad for putting yourself first in your healing, you have a choice as to whether they are worthy of being in your life. You always have a choice, no matter who that person is, so ask yourself if they help you feel good about yourself or not; your outer world reflects your inner world and how you feel about yourself.

I also want to mention here the importance of giving yourself time to integrate healing. Healing cannot be rushed and it cannot be controlled with our rational minds, so give yourself permission to rest, pause and stop when you need to. I know from personal experience of therapy and seeing it with my coaching clients that the healing takes place in between sessions. The magic is in the space in between 'doing' so allow yourself to 'be'. I have to remind myself often that I am a human 'being' not a human 'doing', which means I need rest. I have to remind myself to give myself permission. So, if this resonates with you – give yourself the permission to go slow and take it at your own pace. Allow yourself the space you need to release, change and grow. This is the space where healing can take place, exactly how and when you need it to.

HEALING TOOLKIT

Supporting Survivors

To the supporter - it's okay to not know what to say, and there are things that you could say that are harmful – which is why most times, saying nothing is better than saying anything.

Things Not to Say

I don't believe you/that.
Just get over it.
Don't let it control you.
I know what you mean …
I understand.
Stop talking about it now.
That can't be true.

If you don't know what to say or do – be honest and say that, but also say you want to help and ask them what would be helpful.

Suggested Things to Say When You Don't Know What to Say

We are all unique, so ask your loved one what they need or what helps them. It is not uncommon for them to not know what will help, so offer to explore what could help together. What they most need during their healing is to know they have control, they are loved, and they are safe.

I believe you.
I love you.
You are safe now.
I am here with you.
It wasn't your fault.
I am listening.
You don't have to tell me now – I'm here when you are ready.
I can see it's difficult for you right now...what will help you just for now?
Shall we write down the things that help you feel calm/happy/relaxed for the times you need it? (Help during these times by reminding them and doing these activities with them.)
I will sit with you in silence until you know what you need/want.
I am so glad you are here in this world. (Write down the reasons why the world is a better place because of them.)
I will wait until you feel ready.

Five Ways You Can Help

A common experience of supporters is frustration and feeling helpless seeing a loved one in emotional pain – this is completely under-standable and comes from a well-intentioned place of wanting to help. Keep in mind that this is their process and one that is necessary to move through. The fact that you are wanting to go through it with them will mean so much but, remember, you can't 'fix' it.

The National Association for Adults Abused in Childhood (NAPAC) give the following 5 top tips for supporters to help their loved ones:

1. Take care of yourself in this process.
2. Educate yourself to better understand the impact of abuse and potential triggers.
3. Communicate – learn from your loved one what they need. Avoid trying to control or patronise, learn how to empower the sur-vivor to take back their own power and control.
4. Be considerate – consider who is best placed to support your loved one.
5. No excuse for bad behaviour – anger can be a typical emotion that a survivor will experience during healing but remember that this does not excuse harmful behav-iour towards you.

Journal Prompts for the Supporter

- ○ How do you feel today?

- ○ What effect is this process having upon you?

- ○ How can you best support your loved one?

- ○ How can you be kind to yourself during the hard days?

- ○ What are the tools or activities that can help you both on the bad days?

- ○ How can you both celebrate the good days?

- ○ What do you need to help you?

Journal Prompts for the Survivor

- ○ How can your loved one best support you on the bad days?

- ○ What do you most need today? Communicate the answer to your loved one.

- ○ When you aren't able to express what you need/how you feel in words – how else could you do this?

- ○ What do you need from your loved ones to support you on this healing journey?

- ○ What does your loved one need to know to feel able to help/support you? Ask them what they need and express what you need.

Useful Resources

Useful pages for both survivors and their loved ones – research what services are available locally. Some organisations offer support groups/therapy sessions for supporters of survivors.

National Association for People Abuse in Childhood (NAPAC):
https://napac.org.uk/know-a-survivor/

Recovering from Sexual Violence (RAINN):
https://www.rainn.org/recovering-sexual-violence.
This is an American organisation - I found their supporter page useful.

Conclusion

Dear older Stacie,

I have been listening and feel so grateful that you heard my cries for help and for you to come back for me. What a journey it has been so far. It was a lonely journey for both of us in the beginning. We were both in separate prisons that were cold, dark and scary depths of desolation. I'm so glad we are together to carry onwards with this journey.

We found peace, yes, but the biggest treasure uncovered was our connection to self and finding the resources we had inside all along. It was our bravery and strength that started the journey and combined with determination and tenacity, we now have all we need to achieve and thrive. We didn't deserve what happened; the healing process has given me the understanding and belief that it wasn't my fault. There isn't a fairy tale ending but something even better: self-

> *love and freedom from the fear of emotional pain.*
> *There is no me without you, we are home.*

....

The process of writing this book has been similar to the healing journey itself.

It's nothing like you imagine it to be. I had this vision of it being an elaborate process with big dramatic steps with fanfare, but this was far from the reality. It was the small, consistent and unremarkable efforts that add up to progress. It isn't linear with a manual of 'do this' to get 'here'. It is messy, it requires grit to get through the self-doubt and mental stories, but it is in the 'showing up' daily and honouring the process that you get where you need (and want) to be. There is this point somewhere in the middle (a few actually) when you doubt it all and think it's all pointless because you're not getting anywhere – this is when you're being pushed out of your comfort zone, looking fear in the face. This is the point of 'breaking down' to get to the breakthrough. This is the point testing your dedication to the process. This is the point you need to love yourself more. Things start making sense and the clouds begin to part, letting the light in, revealing the efforts of your hard work.

Deep suffering can often trigger a deeper knowing and connection to self – if you are willing to meet the challenge of facing the painful past, to strive to create a better future. You are a brave soul, no matter where you are today. Your only job for today is to choose you – choose to want more than you received from the past. You are your own healer. You are worthy despite what the inner critic will try to convince you of otherwise.

Ten years ago, I didn't even know I was on a healing journey. I can't tell you exactly when it started; I just felt alone, scared, and emotionally numb. I could never have imagined that 10 years later I would be here writing a book about healing after sexual trauma. What I did know was that I couldn't continue to live life in survival mode, just going through life as a robot. My heart was closed off to prevent it from getting hurt even more, but what I have come to learn is that it also meant it was closed off from love – love for myself and from others. I know why I did this and I am so grateful for the tenacity of my younger self for persevering and pushing me forward to seek the ways that could bring inner peace and a sense of self again.

That's the thing about healing, sometimes it's only with hindsight that we can see our progress and realise it has begun and that it is 'in progress'. The one thing I can be certain of now is that there isn't an end date of when I will be 'healed'; it isn't a destination. Healing is a state of being; it is wellbeing. For me, it is a sense of being able to think back to that time in my life and not be triggered of the painful emotions. I look back with pride for my progress and gratitude for having the courage and tenacity to put myself first and wanting more from my life. It doesn't happen overnight and it does require a commitment to self to want more than where you are right now. You are in control of when that journey starts.

You are on your way.

There is no grand finale in this process but celebrate the progress. It is important you know the new feeling you are seeking as an indicator that you are living a life after sexual trauma; what it would feel like or what your life would look like?

What are the steps in between? How can you measure progress?

This is different for each of us but what is important is your progress and what it feels/looks like for you. Celebrate your progress, no matter how small it may seem. Progress is progress.

We are all on our way in this life in our own unique way.

Life is the big picture journey and unfolds over time. Healing after sexual trauma is a journey within a journey and will unfold as you do. It is important to reflect on this progress in a way that is meaningful to you.

There are many healing modalities that you can explore.

My invitation to you is to explore. Explore what feels good for you.

- Breathwork
- Energy healing
- Journaling
- Talking therapy
- Yoga
- Movement
- Painting
- Dancing

Any form of self-expression that feels right for you will be your way to healing yourself.

I wrote this book for those that feel they can't yet speak their truth.

I wrote this book to encourage you to be your fullest truest expression of you – because there is no one like you in this world.

You deserve so much more than life has given you so far. You can take back control of your life by choosing yourself, by choosing to heal.

At the foundation of this book, it is an invitation for you to feel safe enough to listen inwards. Tune into yourself, you are your own healer. The answers are never out 'there'; they are within you. You have everything you need – you just need to find the treasures that lie within. It is a process of feeling safe, so it's okay if you don't believe this right now. A process that unfolds when you are ready and at a pace that is right for you. There is so much to uncover – getting to know who you really are and finding your worth. It all starts with a belief that there is something there within you worth exploring.

You are worthy.
More than you know right now.
Be curious for what is possible.
Trust yourself.
It is safe now, my darling.

The big question is, can you 'get over' sexual abuse?

I believe you can move through it but that we ultimately carry it with us, but in a way that it doesn't any longer have any power over us. I know that my experience is intrinsically a part of me – it most definitely does not define me and it is not my identity or who I am; however, it has shaped my life, sending me on a quest to find myself. 'Letting go' was something I focused on a lot during my days of therapy – I so desperately wanted to magically 'just let it go'. One thing I found was the more I focused on 'letting go', it didn't happen. It stuck to me even more – I felt stuck even more. When I realised that I needed to surrender to my process, letting go organically happened. What did I let go of? I didn't let go of the trauma itself because it's a part of my story, but what I did let go of was the guilt and shame that held me back from healing. Healing is not a process we can control or shape to be what we want it to be, but we can take back our control by choosing to show up for ourselves and commit to healing one day at a time.

No one else can define your experience or what your healing 'should' look like – it is yours and yours only. So, what do you want to do with it? What do you want from your life?

*~ Healing is the way to
transform pain into power. ~*

I am not trying to simplify or minimise the work and grit it takes to heal after sexual abuse. It is messy, hard work and tiring (to name a few), but it is also worth it, powerful, transformational, and it is also beautifully yours to feel proud of.

Release expectations for what it 'should' be like or what it might look like – allow it to unfold exactly as it's meant to. You are exactly where you are meant to be, even if you don't feel that right now.

The possibilities are endless – don't be held back by what your past has delivered or by the confines of limiting thoughts within the mind. So, if you made it this far into the book, I know you want to be free from how your experience of trauma has made you feel. You want more. You deserve more.

It is possible – the first step is believing that it is possible and that you deserve it.

Set the intention that you want to release what is holding you back from being your fullest, truest expression of your beautiful self – to release what is no longer serving you. Start where you are now, even if you don't feel ready. The truth is, we never feel ready. But then we were never ready for what happened to us in the first place but we survived. If you survived them days, weeks, months, or years, then I promise you that you will survive the healing process.

You deserve more in this life than you previously received.

You deserve a life *after* sexual trauma.

There *is* life after sexual abuse – the question is, what do you want it to be?

My Healing Journey: The Unknown Quest

Ten years ago, I set off on a journey with an idea of what I wanted – to be 'fixed'. There wasn't a map or manual to follow but I had this idea that maybe it was like going to a physical destination, like going on a plane to somewhere new and magical. Where miracles happen and people return all happy and sparkly new, ready to carry on with the rest of their lives. The thing was, I tried to set on this journey several times but fear rose up within me and told me to stay put until I found out what would happen when I got 'there'. The fear of the unknown kept me frozen. Frozen within my mental prison of self-loathing desolation.

One day, seeing someone else's courage to face their fear sparked something inside me – it was the accumulation of all the previous attempts that were now enough to move me forward towards action. I didn't know where this destination was, but I packed a bag with a few things that I thought may help on my journey. I was heading outside of my comfort zone. I came to learn that the fear of being outside my comfort zone was a sign that the undulating path would be worth it and I would become a different version of myself by the time I got there.

The question is, where is there?

I started the physical journey to find 'healing' – the elusive grand destination. That path led me not to a geographical location outside of myself, but actually, I realised the only way through was inwards. The healing journey was about the inner quest – truly seeing what was inside and who I really was. Learning to love all parts of myself. The parts that I previously thought were unlovable. So, I closed my eyes and I tapped into that part of myself that just knew – I felt it in my body.

That's when I realised it's not about having the perfect map to tell you where to go, but instead it's about trusting in the unknown and allowing the journey to take you where you need to be – because there's a part of us that always knows. To know that life is about being curious; curious about the unknown and allowing the magic to be revealed to us instead of trying to control the outcome.

We just need to be brave enough to take the journey and leap into the unknown and to believe that we have everything we need inside of us.

What I did find along my journey was self-belief, self-love and hope for the future. A future without fear of raw painful emotions falling out. The inner quest doesn't end in a final destination. The quest is forever unfolding and evolving because I am always growing and changing and that's okay. I am becoming – becoming whole because I realise I was never broken. I am reclaiming the pieces of me that were wrongfully taken.

I chose myself – I chose self-worth.

How to Move Forward

If you are reading this book, you're already moving forward to seek ways to heal.

However you chose to read it, I hope that it will be a helpful companion to support you where you are and for where you are going on your healing journey. I hope this book has given you permission to honour where you are now and given you hope for moving forward positively to how you want to feel and where you want to be.

You can come back to the sections when you are at that particular stage in your own process – sometimes it is obvious, such as when we are going through talking therapy, and other times it is subtle – because our mind, body and soul are all interconnected. Allow your process to be what it needs to be and give yourself permission to be 'messy' and not have it all together. The reality is, no one 'has it all together' with life all worked out, and so bring kindness and compassion to yourself. This is hard enough without the inner critic ruling with critical thoughts as well.

If resistance comes up when reading, know that this is not uncommon; it can be an indication of where you need to look closer within yourself. Resistance can show up in many ways, such as a horrible gut feeling or denial. Being able to notice resistance is a great place to be – I invite you to write down what brought up that resistance and ask yourself what specifically is causing it to rise up in you. Therapists are good at noticing resistance and can guide you to explore this at your own pace. If you are further along on your healing journey, then self-directed writing therapy (journaling) is a way to explore this yourself.

Resource Toolkit

The Survivors Trust

www.thesurvivorstrust.org

The Survivors Trust is the largest umbrella agency for specialist rape and sexual abuse services in the UK.

Mind Charity

www.mind.org.uk

The charity 'Mind' has a useful resources page listing the national support services for survivors of sexual abuse, which is a great place to start your search, and from there you can search within your locality for further support.

The National Association for People Abused in Childhood (NAPAC)

www.napac.org.uk

NAPAC offers support to adult survivors of all

types of childhood abuse, including physical, sexual, emotional abuse or neglect.

Survivors UK

www.survivorsuk.org

A charity supporting men following rape and sexual assault, challenging silence and attitudes.

Dr Nina Burrowes

www.ninaburrowes.com

Nina is a psychologist who is passionate about helping people understand the psychology of child sexual abuse, sexual harassment and domestic abuse. She has several illustrated books and videos to explain why abuse happens, what the impact of abuse is, how to support people and what we can all do to prevent it.

The Courage to be me: a story of courage, self-compassion and hope after rape or sexual abuse – this is a book that I found helpful during my early days of understanding why I felt like I felt. It makes a huge difference when we realise we aren't alone in how we feel and that the feelings are 'normal' and valid.

Books

Dr Nicole LePera (The Holistic Psychologist)
How to Do the Work: Recognise your patterns, heal from your past and create your Self. This work is a shift from traditional psychotherapy to a more holistic approach to empower self-healing.

Bessel van der Kolk: *The Body Keeps the Score: Mind, Brain and Body in the Transformation of Trauma.*

Penny Parks: *Rescuing the Inner Child: Therapy for Adults Sexually Abused as Children.*

Sarah Blondin: *Heart Minded: How to hold Yourself and Others in Love.*

Sarah is also a Meditation teacher on Insight Timer app and has been a pivotal and loving voice during my healing through her meditations.

Louise L. Hay: *You Can Heal Your Life.*

Other Louise Hay resources – I found these card decks useful during my therapy days to give me something positive to focus upon and to explore self-love. I picked a card each day and its quite nice to journal on the affirmation too and what it means to you.

- *Power Thought Cards* – a deck of 64 cards with affirmations to inspire a new way of thinking and open up new possibilities.

- *How to Love Yourself Cards* – a deck of 64 affirmations for self-love

An online resource: *Pregnancy, birth and Parenthood after Childhood Sexual Abuse* (June 2019): www.thesurvivorstrust.org/pbpaftercsa

Connect with Me

I love nothing more than hearing from other survivors who feel empowered to heal themselves from their trauma. There are several ways you can connect with me if you wish to:

My Website
www.Stacie-Glass.com
You can sign up for my newsletter to download the PDF version of the 'Things I wish I had known 10 years ago' and 'Them Days': SOS Self-Care worksheets: **www.stacie-glass.com/lifeaftersexualabuse**

Facebook
Life after sexual abuse blog:
www.facebook.com/CSAblog/

Instagram
@_StacieGlass_
#lifeaftersexualabuse

HEALING TOOLKIT

Things I Wish I Had Known 10 Years Ago

These could be used as affirmations for what you most need during the challenging times of healing. You can write them out and put them up where you can see them. Be as creative as you want such as using colours that you love or using them as doodles/art. Change it to the present tense, i.e., I am safe, I am loved.

....

You deserve to heal

You are not your trauma

Start where you are – even if you don't feel ready

I believe you

It's okay if you feel lost

It's okay if some days you're just surviving

It's okay to pause when you need to

You are important and you matter

You are safe

You are loved

You are worth it

Your past doesn't define your worth

It wasn't your fault

Healing is messy – allow it to be what you need, not

what you think it should be

All your emotions and needs are valid

Your boundaries are important and deserve respect

You are allowed to say no

You are in control

You can give yourself what you need

You do not need to do this alone

You are worthy of the love and support right here

where you are

You are human

You are doing better than you think

You are enough – exactly as you are

You are not broken

Everything you feel is valid

You are stronger than you know

Feel it all – the only way out is through

You are already brave

You deserve freedom from the past

Just for today …

You are not selfish for putting yourself first

Your needs are as important as anyone else's

Your voice matters – it is safe to speak your truth

There is beauty within the mess – see your beauty

You are your own healer

The answers are within you

It's okay if you can't just 'let it go'

This too shall pass

Your best today is enough

Just for today, release the negative self-talk

The future isn't yet written

Forgive yourself for the past

Practice self-forgiveness daily

It was bad enough – don't keep yourself hostage in your thoughts now

You do not need to apologise for being who you are/ how you are

You don't need to feel your feelings *all the time* to heal

HEALING TOOLKIT

'Them Days': SOS Self-Care

For the days when it's all too much

Some days during healing, all we can do is just about survive – these are the days I encourage you to be gentle with yourself and keep that inner critic in check.

This page is the place you can refer back to remind you of SOS self-care for these tough days. If you feel comfortable to, share it with your loved ones so they know what they can do to help you too.

Write here a reminder that you need to read on these days:

Write here a favourite quote:

Create a music playlist of the songs that help to uplift you and make you smile.

Create a music playlist of the songs that help you release emotions – it's okay to cry/scream /let out sounds. It's good to let it all out.

Write a list here of activities that make you feel good, i.e., having a warm bath, eating ice cream, playing with your beloved pet, reading a book, watching a favourite film, singing out loud and proud, etc.

Write down the people you can reach out to today, who you can be completely as you are with:

Write a letter to your future self – seal it in an envelope and put a date on it that you want to open it in the future.

Write some words to yourself as if you are your best friend – what would they say to you today?

Today, I will do more of ...

Today, I will do less of ...

What are you looking forward to in the future?
If you can't find something, take a small step
towards creating something to look forward to.

Acknowledgements

I would not be here if it was not for my inner warrior – my inner child.

Her tenacity and strength inspired this book.

Thank you to my husband, Russell. Your capacity to love and support me inspires me every day. With you, I feel fully supported to be my authentic self.

Katherine, my brave sister, thank you for showing me what it means to be courageous. It was you who gave me the final nudge to move forward on my healing journey and ultimately to choose me.

RSVP – thank you for your unwavering belief and compassion and, of course, many years of support. I am so grateful I had access to such an amazing service that sadly many do not. You make such a difference to so many lives.

Natalie - my therapist from RSVP, you have a special place in my heart for the years you held space for me. You are a big reason for how I got to where I am now. I hope you realise the impact you have upon your clients' lives. I will be forever grateful for your professional (and personal) nurturing and belief in me.

George Lizos, thank you for seeing value in this book and your support through this process. Thank you to That Guy's House for the opportunity to put my voice out into the world. We will not be silenced by abuse nor abusers.

Kathryn Gutteridge, thank you for all your unending hard work advocating for survivors, your support for this book and your kind words.

Thank you to all those who have supported me along this journey, your support and love is what has kept me going when at times it has felt like society doesn't want to talk about sexual abuse.

Thank you to those who have fallen out of my life during my journey – you showed me where I lacked self-worth and needed greater boundaries to put myself first.

Lastly, but not least– thank you to you, the reader, for being here. If you are a survivor, I salute you for your ability to survive the darkest of days. If you are supporting a survivor – thank you for you showing us that we are worthy of love.

About the Author

Stacie Glass is a survivor of childhood sexual abuse, midwife, Reiki practitioner and an NLP and emotional well-being coach. A passionate advocate for sexual abuse survivors and their right to a life after sexual trauma, one free of shame and guilt. Stacie has a wealth of experience in the National Health Service (NHS) as a registered midwife and in healthcare governance and regulation. She has always been interested in psychology and mental/emotional wellbeing and completed a master's degree in health research, completing a project into the effectiveness of screening tools for mental health issues during pregnancy.

Stacie has been on her healing journey since 2011 which has led her to explore and understand how sexual trauma impacts the mind, body and soul, whilst doing the inner work herself. She feels very strongly that survivors know that they are not what happened to them – they are worthy of a life free of the shackles of sexual abuse.

Living in West Sussex UK but originally from Birmingham - a 'Brummie' girl at heart – Stacie loves living near the sea and walking through the vast natural beauty of the south east of England. Her healing journey and self-discovery revealed a deep capacity to hold space for others and their growth in finding their own inner wisdom that lies within.

www.stacie-glass.com

@_StacieGlass_

Lightning Source UK Ltd.
Milton Keynes UK
UKHW021401130921
390500UK00015B/1252